AWAITING A SAVIOR

The Gospel, the New Creation and the End of Poverty

Aaron Armstrong
Cruciform Press | Released October, 2011

To Ayax, whose love for the poor and love for
the Lord is both humbling and inspiring.
– Aaron Armstrong

CruciformPress

"Aaron Armstrong's heart to minister to the least of these is on full display in this concise book about the opportunities and limitations of ministry to the poor. Challenging our own idolatry, our own motivations, and our own actions, *Awaiting a Savior* reorients our mercy ministry around the gospel, seeking to show how a life of love is the overflow of a grace-filled heart."

Trevin Wax, editor of *TGM* (Theology, Gospel, Mission) and author of *Counterfeit Gospels* and *Holy Subversion*

"Aaron Armstrong has not only *thought hard* about alleviating poverty, he's also *worked hard* at it. Consequently, this biblical theology of poverty is a mixture of pessimism, optimism, and realism. He's rightly pessimistic about humanistic solutions, he's brightly optimistic about God's ultimate solution, and he's practically realistic about the best and most the Church can do in this present age."

Dr. David P. Murray, professor, Puritan Reformed Theological Seminary; president of HeadHeartHand Media

"Finally, a book that tackles the subject of poverty in a biblical, balanced, thought-provoking, and convicting manner! In his book, Aaron manages to walk the fine line of calling for a biblical solution to poverty without causing the reader to feel overly burdened with unnecessary, unbiblical guilt. He also shows how biblical generosity is ultimately rooted in the generosity of God himself. Too many times I've seen the call for generosity fueled by legalistic guilt. Aaron instead points the reader to the glories of the gospel as the motivation for giving. Read this book. Discuss it with your friends. Be generous!"

Stephen Altrogge, author of *The Greener Grass Conspiracy*; pastor; blogger at TheBlazingCenter.com

"While many books on eradicating poverty focus solely on statistics and need as motivating tactics, Awaiting a Savior moves beyond the stats, the great need, and excellently emphasizes addressing the root of poverty and what motivates us to adress the issue. The redemptive story of God highlighted in this book provides the grace-based motivation in the gospel necessary to provide the most holistic and sustainable response to the great need around us. Few books so astutely combine a comprehensive theological look at poverty with empowering, inspirational motivation."

Logan Gentry, Pastor of Community & Justice, Apostles Church, NYC

"In his book, *Awaiting a Savior*, Aaron Armstrong addresses the issue of poverty in a clear and theologically practical way. Armstrong does a good job emphasizing sin's damaging effects on economics and pointing to the one true hope of the world, Jesus. This book is a valuable resource to help Christians think biblically when it comes to finances, economics, resources, and poverty."

Pastor Bubba Jennings, Mars Hill Church, Seattle, WA

"In our highly activist, solutions-oriented generation, we easily think that we ourselves are the solution to the world's social ills, particularly poverty. But the problem of poverty is the problem of sin and its solution lies in the heart of the gospel. Aaron Armstrong brilliantly brings us back to Genesis and delivers a theologically robust vision for obeying the Scriptures' command to help the poor while living in anxious anticipation of Christ's coming Kingdom."

Daniel Darling, Senior Pastor of Gages Lake Bible Church; author, *iFaith: Connecting to God in the 21st Century*

"We all care about poverty, but caring isn't enough. We need to move beyond feelings and good intentions. In *Awaiting a Savior,* Aaron Armstrong helps us think theologically about poverty, because we'll never know how to respond until we understand both the issue and our response from a biblical perspective. He then shows us how we can respond out of grace, not guilt. This book is a clear and insightful look at an issue that's on all of our minds."

Darryl Dash, pastor, blogger at DashHouse.com

"Aaron Armstrong has succeeded in helping us see the solution to poverty in a biblical light. He understands that poverty itself is no more a root problem than those things said to be born out of it, such as economic oppression or social injustice. Thus, he calls us back to Scripture to see that the real root problem is sin and that the answer is found in nothing less than the enduring good news of Jesus Christ. With so much confusion in the Church and para-church ministries regarding a Christian response to poverty and so much interest in social justice presently, this volume is an urgent read for any Christian who has a genuine interest in helping the poor."

N. D. Muscutt, Pastor, Newcastle Fellowship Baptist Church

"Awaiting a Savior is a compelling and captivating book that looks at global poverty through the wide-angle lens of the gospel. Aaron Armstrong's book will likely change the way you look at the problem of poverty in our world and how you think about addressing it. But what I love most about Awaiting a Savior is that it empowers us to care for the poor by making much of Jesus."

Dan Cruver, author of *Reclaiming Adoption*, director of Together for Adoption

"Aaron Armstrong's book, *Awaiting A Savior*, brings a fresh approach to the world-wide problem of poverty. It is gospel-driven, Jesus-centered, and gets at the real but often overlooked cause of poverty. This is not another book that takes you on a guilt trip becuase we're 'not doing enough.' It is not filled with lists of all the things we should do to eliminate poverty, but rather is a solid theological treatment of what poverty really stems from and how to see it within a biblical framework. Aaron has provided thought provoking questions throughout that will get your brain churning."

Pastor Dave Kraft, Mars Hill Church, Orange County, CA; author of *Leaders Who Last*

Table of Contents

Cruciform**Press**
something new in Christian publishing

Our Books: Short. Clear. Concise. Helpful. Inspiring. Gospel-focused. *Print, ebook, audiobook.*

Monthly Releases: A new book the first day of every month.

Consistent Prices: Every book costs the same.

Subscription Options: Print books or ebooks delivered to you every month, at a discount. Or buy one at a time.

Annual or Monthly Subscriptions

Print Book . . . . $6.49 per month
Ebook　 . . . . $3.99 per month

Non-Subscription Sales

1-5 Print Books . . . . $8.45 each
6-50 Print Books . . . . $7.45 each
More than 50 Print Books . . . . $6.45 each

---

Awaiting a Savior: The Gospel, the New Creation and the End of Poverty

Print ISBN:　　　　　　978-1-936760-32-9
ePub ISBN:　　　　　　978-1-936760-34-3
Mobipocket ISBN:　　　978-1-936760-33-6

Introduction
THE REAL ISSUE

"What's the real issue?"

The question on the billboard had done its job. "I wonder what that's about?" I asked my wife. "Not sure," she replied. "Maybe you should go to the website." And later that day I sat down at the computer to learn what, exactly, was the real issue.

Apparently, it's poverty.

I read that, despite living in one of the richest cities in one of the wealthiest countries in the world, almost one in five children here in London, Ontario is born into poverty. Seventeen percent of citizens can't afford to buy groceries or keep a roof over their heads.[1] I began to imagine: could it be that one of every five families we know doesn't have enough food or is in danger of becoming homeless?

"What am I supposed to do about this?" I wondered as I read on. Here's what the site recommended:

1. Give your time and resources to local aid groups, like food banks and local initiatives that provide basic needs such as food, baby items, storage space, and clothing.

2.   Advocate for change in government policies.
3.   Engage in discussion online about solutions and what you think is or isn't working in current policies.[2]

Give, talk to the government, and engage with others over these issues. Do these responses get at the core of the issue?

This kind of clear, simple, action-oriented advice is found in much of the talk about poverty. Actions like these can have value, but you don't have to look too hard to see that especially on a global scale, people are already giving a lot of money and talking a great deal about poverty. Experts like Jeffrey Sachs and Paul Collier are writing about the causes of and solutions to poverty. Hundreds — more likely, *thousands* — of charitable organizations large and small are raising awareness regarding the poor and seeking to bring them relief. Even rock star/activist Bono has gotten into the mix. His organization, ONE, hopes to get the First World to cancel Third World debt and provide additional relief dollars to impoverished nations.[3]

Of course, most people who focus on poverty see it as wrapped up in larger questions of injustice and inequality. Yet the proposed solutions remain the same: resource distribution, awareness, and effort. Do we just need more of all three? If we can distribute resources differently, put the right government and private-sector policies in place, and shift some of our personal and social priorities, shall all be well?

This perspective, however well-intentioned, is fundamentally flawed. We *should* have a heart of generosity toward the poor, and there is certainly a place for giving.

We can and should commend the work of many of the organizations seeking to serve and support the poor. As Christians, we should be compassionate toward the poor and pray for them. And it is always worth evaluating whether government policies are helping or hurting.

But, especially as Christians, we need to be very clear about something. Resources and awareness and policies are important, but poverty is not fundamentally *about* any of these things.

The root cause of poverty is sin.

Don't conclude too quickly that you know precisely what I mean by this statement, or that you understand exactly what applications should follow from it. This apparently simple sentence is just the beginning of a complicated conversation.

The Problem at the Heart of Poverty

Everywhere you look, there is evil—lying, murder, theft, adultery, abuse, apathy, and all the rest. You cannot turn on the TV or radio or go online without being confronted by sin. And sin is not simply something we do—it's part of who we are. You and I, along with every human who has ever lived, are born sinners.[4] Before we take our first breath, we are ruled by sin. We love it and are naturally its slaves.

Yet the pervasiveness and nature of sin is missing completely from most of today's discussion surrounding poverty. The idea that we can wipe out injustice and inequality for good overlooks the fundamental problem of our sinful nature. Therefore, the basic premise of this book is that *our good faith efforts to address legitimate questions of poverty and injustice must never lose sight of the fact that poverty will persist as long as the heart of man is ruled by sin.*

Christians can often overlook this as well as unbelievers can, which leads to even more confusion. Some of us hold to a theology declaring that it is our mandate as the Church to bring about the end of poverty. Others, holding a different theology, seem content to do nothing at all and wait for Christ to return. Neither approach is acceptable.

I wrote this book because I am among those who believe that the Bible's teaching on poverty is clear and carries clear implications for us as Christians. We need to be able to think about and respond to these issues biblically. I hope to show that the best way to help the poor is to minister to them as the Church, in both word and deed, to the glory of God.

This is no academic exercise for me. As an employee of a Christian charity that works with the Church to care for the poor, I have seen real poverty firsthand—and I have seen the rich hope that the gospel brings to those who live in it. As a husband and father, I am eager to teach my family how we can respond faithfully and effectively to the needs of the poor—economic needs, spiritual needs, human needs.

I have hope that there is a biblical and effective way for the Church to serve the poor. I want you to have that hope as well. As Christians, we don't have the option to ignore true poverty, and we must not waste our time and resources on approaches that ignore the pervasive presence of sin in every heart.

When I look at poverty, I do not feel defeated. When I see the needs of the world, I am not disheartened. When I weigh the clear responsibilities we have to care for the poor,[5] I am not overwhelmed. I know there are things we can do to serve the poor, that God will give us grace to do them, and that he will take pleasure in our efforts—where we succeed and even where we fail.

I also know that hope for truly resolving the injustices of this world is not to be found in utopian visions of global partnership, or pouring massive amounts of money into relief efforts, or even in providing food, education, and opportunities to people who don't have them. While we are responsible for pursuing biblical solutions to poverty, our only hope for an *ultimate* solution is in the return of Christ, when *he* will put an end once and for all to sin, suffering, and death, and bring about the new creation. That's the hope I want to share with you in this book.

Reflect, Discuss, Apply

1. Before you picked up this book, what was your perspective on poverty in general and how Christians should respond? Write a paragraph summarizing your thoughts. If you're in a group study, share what you've written with your group.
2. Have you ever been or are you currently involved

with any organization serving the poor in your community? What would you say is the goal of that organization?

3. Have you traveled to the developing world as part of a short-term missions group? If so, what have you learned from those experiences?

4. The author writes that the real issue behind poverty lies within the heart of man. Do you agree? Explain your answer.

5. Read Psalm 51:1-6. What does David say about man's state?

6. What is at least one thing you hope to take away from this study?

One
POVERTY IS SPIRITUAL

The Persistence of Sin

Some of the best moments in parenthood happen when you see that your efforts to teach your children to become civilized human beings are actually paying off. One day they can do almost nothing on their own. But in a few short years they are dressing themselves, practicing the alphabet, praying, coloring, and expressing distinct preferences about breakfast foods. Without instruction and example, children would learn almost none of this. They must be taught.

But there's one thing no parent ever has to teach: how to lie. It seems to be a natural talent (if you can call it that) — no instruction necessary, no assembly required. Lies, gossip, slander, mockery, and showing off come so easily to us that they seem almost instinctual, as if we were made to do them. Yet, as we examine the Scriptures, we learn something very different. These things that seem so natural are not the result of how we were made. They're the result of a curse.

How the Curse Came

How *were* we created in the beginning? Where did this curse come from? And what does it mean for our study of the roots of poverty? To answer these questions, we need to start, as the Scriptures do—at the beginning.

The opening of the book of Genesis describes the creation of the universe. Over the course of six days, God literally spoke the world into existence—light and darkness, day and night, land and sea, plant and animals, the sun and moon and stars—everything.[6] As each new creation emerged, God "saw that it was good."[7] There was no flaw, fault, or error. All was exactly as God desired it to be. Then, God spoke again, creating the first humans. But when he speaks this time, he says something different. He doesn't say, "I will make man according to *their* kinds," as he did with plants and with animals. He says, "Let us make man in *our image*, after *our likeness*."[8]

Put simply, God made humans to be fundamentally different than the rest of creation. We were given "dominion . . . over all the earth" and everything in it. We were called to "fill the earth and subdue it."[9] Humans were intended to be more than just another part of the created order. No other creature was given this command to govern and steward the earth. Man and woman were intended to represent God in the place he had made for them.

With the creation of the first man and woman, God saw "everything that he had made, and behold, it was very good."[10] The divine work of creation was now complete. Genesis chapter two leaves us with a picture of the "very good"-ness of creation as the man and the woman enjoy

hip with one another, with the rest of
: importantly with their Creator.[11] *It*
ich poverty could not exist. A world free
relational, or spiritual need. It's the
_____ ...g for today.

In this perfect world, there was only one rule, found
in Genesis 2:16-17: "You may surely eat of every tree of
the garden, but of the tree of the knowledge of good and
evil you shall not eat, for in the day that you eat of it you
shall surely die." We don't know how many days, months,
or years passed, but for some time Adam and Eve obeyed
that single command. Then the serpent came, a cunning
creature that was no mere reptile. He was apparently the
devil himself,[12] come with one agenda: to tempt God's
image-bearers to reject their Creator.

What makes the serpent so cunning is that he doesn't
grandstand. His technique for tempting Adam and Eve to
disobey God is subtle and understated. He starts by simply
slithering up to the woman and starting a conversation.

"Did God actually say, 'You shall not eat of *any* tree in
the garden'?" the serpent asks.[13] At first glance, it almost
sounds like the serpent is merely asking for clarification.
But something else is going on. God had made a ruling
about *one single tree*. By suggesting that God's prohibi-
tion extended to *every* tree, the serpent misrepresents
God. He also positions Eve to begin to think differently
about God and his commands. That's the way temptation
is: subtle, multi-layered, and easy to miss.

The serpent's temptation leads Eve to fix her eyes
on what she *doesn't* have—freedom to eat of the fruit of

this one tree—rather than on all that God has graciously provided,[14] and this discontentment gives the serpent his opportunity to strike. You can almost hear the twisted delight in his voice as he says, "You will not surely die. For God knows that when you eat of it your eyes will be opened, and you will be like God, knowing good and evil."[15]

With Eve already contemplating disobedience, the serpent gives her a final incentive to sin: *she will be like God*. If she does the one thing she is forbidden from doing (eating from that particular tree) she will have the one thing she does not now possess: a supposed equality with God—the God who suddenly seems so unreasonable and oppressive.

All it took was a single question—a conversation starter—to move Eve along the serpent's train of thought. She went from devoted follower and faithful friend of God to not merely doubting God's goodness, but wanting to be like him.

> So when the woman saw that the tree was good for food, and that it was a delight to the eyes, and that the tree was to be desired to make one wise, she took of its fruit and ate, and she also gave some to her husband who was with her, and he ate. Then the eyes of both were opened, and they knew that they were naked.[16]

This is how sin entered the world. God's image bearers chose to believe the lie that they could be "like God"— equal to him, and therefore not subject to his commands.

It's the same lie we believe today, appearing in

countless different manifestations and touching every aspect of our lives. We want to wrestle control of our destinies away from God. Being the only creatures called to exercise dominion on God's behalf isn't quite enough for us. We don't want to settle for being God's representatives, we want to be more "like God" than that—we want control. (As we will discuss later, this desire to force outcomes and control destinies has come to dominate much of the antipoverty movement.)

The result of Adam and Eve's disobedience was just as God had predicted: "you shall surely die." Death came, suddenly and swiftly, even if physical death was not immediate. Spiritually, the man and the woman died in their trespasses and sins, becoming children of wrath, enslaved to sin.[17] So our inheritance from our first parents became not a life of blessing and joyful fellowship with God, but death and damnation: "sin came into the world through one man, and death through sin, and so death spread to all men because all sinned," wrote the apostle Paul.[18]

Sin destroyed Adam and Eve's relationship with God and devastated their relationship with each other and the rest of creation. They became ashamed of their nakedness and hid themselves, first from one another and then from God when they heard him in the garden. Adam and Eve became different people, fallen sinners, given to evasion and blameshifting and making excuses for their sinful behavior.[19] They not only flagrantly disobeyed God, but they then went on a mission to deny responsibility for their disobedience.

God responded with a curse.

The Curse, Spoken and Manifested

First God cursed the serpent, then Eve, then Adam. All these curses are still in effect, still obvious. For our purposes, we will consider only the curses spoken over Eve and Adam.

<u>The curse upon Eve and relationships.</u> God's curse upon Eve brought great pain in childbearing and a fractured relationship with her husband. "Your desire shall be for your husband, and he shall rule over you," we're told.[20] This part of Eve's curse seems to be about control—a constant jockeying for position that can devastate male-female relationships. Without suggesting that women take exclusive responsibility for relational difficulties, we can certainly see this curse manifested today.

<u>The curse upon Adam and economics.</u> Whereas the curse upon Eve is primarily about interpersonal relationships, Adam's curse spreads outward to all economic life. The ground is cursed because of him, so meeting material needs will be difficult. Fruitfulness will require toil. At every turn, forces from outside will oppose our efforts at material advancement. Prosperity will always be challenging and elusive. The very materials and processes we work with to try to create prosperity will resist us. And it will continue like this until the day we die.[21]

Today, as it has been since the fall of Adam and Eve, all our efforts to provide and prosper meet with opposition. From subsistence farmers in forgotten corners of the globe to CEOs in corner offices, all progress requires toil. The curse on labor is still in effect, and this has extensive implications for how we understand and respond to poverty.

It's also obvious that the excuse-making and blame-shifting we see Adam demonstrating in the Garden continued after the fall, as men frequently fail to take responsibility for their actions or the actions of those under their leadership:

- We see it with Aaron when, after he fashioned a golden calf for the grumbling people of Israel, said to Moses, "I don't know how this calf got here—I just took the gold, threw it in the fire and out came a calf."[22]
- We see it in Eli who failed to correct his sons when they had abused their positions as priests of the people of God.[23]
- We see it with David's messed-up family and his refusal to discipline his children, which led to the rape of his daughter, one son's murder, and another son's attempted coup d'état.[24]
- We even see it today as popular entertainment, which always echoes the culture, features so many sitcoms built around bumbling, bungling, irresponsible men.

Poverty, a Result of the Curse

Adam and Eve's disobedience resulted not in the fulfillment of their desire to be like God but in a curse. Sin backfired, as it always does. The curse is at work continually even today, in more ways than anyone can count, and in every life—no exceptions.

If not for the curse—God's just response to Adam and Eve's fall into sin—and therefore the fact that we face constant opposition as we aim to be productive, we might not even call it "working." Life would be very different—in ways that we may not be able to imagine well until we are with Christ in the new heavens and new earth.

Everything about Adam and Eve's fall makes economic prosperity difficult and elusive. In fact, *the fall has made poverty the default setting*, an ever-present gravitational pull intent on dragging us down. This is true not only because it is now harder to produce material wealth but also because the fall triggered an ongoing cascade of relational challenges characterized by blame-shifting and excuses about our sin, as well as an ongoing desire in each of us to play God over one another. Hardly a recipe for success.

The Difference between Root and Branch

People who study poverty today have a hard job.

First, you must define what poverty is. How poor is poor? There are many levels of poverty, and poverty in North America can look very different, for example, from poverty in West Africa. Then you must consider a huge number of factors to try to figure out what mix of things is really "causing" poverty.

But if you are one of these researchers, you may have an even bigger obstacle before you. If you don't understand what happened in the Garden of Eden, you are missing the single biggest factor that contributes to poverty. You are blind to the fundamental, underlying cause. You can see lots of branches, but you don't realize they all connect to a root. You can recognize many symptoms, but you end up imagining that the symptoms are the disease itself.

Material poverty. For some researchers, poverty is all about what people have or don't have. The focus is on whether a particular society is experiencing economic growth, or whether people have shoes, proper food and shelter, or access to basic medical care.

External factors. Other researchers may include additional factors in their analysis. Is government corruption damaging the economy and preventing the fair distribution of existing resources? Is the country landlocked without any good trade routes, seaports, or airports? Are cycles of civil war and political instability preventing an economy from gaining traction?

It's easy to look at something as ambiguous and complex as poverty and try to define it exclusively in terms of external factors or the lack of material possessions. But when we do that, we are looking only at the effects of sin and the curse, not sin *itself*.

All of this goes back to the curse. Soil that produces few edible plants is a result of the curse. War and corruption and cheating go back to the curse because they are driven by people who, being sinners, want desperately to become rich, powerful, and autonomous—like God.

All poverty has its roots in the curse. Everything else is just branches. Poverty, therefore, is fundamentally a spiritual issue, not a material issue or a matter of policies and systems and government. This is why the solutions that are frequently offered to "solve the poverty problem," even if well-intentioned, can seem insufficient.

Some suggest, for example, that we could end poverty by redistributing wealth: those with more material prosperity would sacrifice in order to bless those who have less. This could be accomplished, we are told, by eliminating the debts of the poorest countries, increasing the aid that richer countries give to poorer ones,[25] and seeking to stimulate the economies of weaker countries. The idea is that this would create a "new normal" for poor countries and give them a fresh start economically.

Others say the solution must come from within the poor nation itself. Poverty can only end if the society trapped in it *wants* to change, although we can encourage them to help themselves through aid, security, trade, and better laws and charters.[26]

These ideas are not all bad. Some even follow biblical principles of compassion and generosity. It is certainly possible to do some good by using these approaches. But nowhere in these analyses is the root problem of sin taken into account.

If it is true, as I have suggested, that the Bible teaches that poverty is the result of sin and the curse, these solutions are treating symptoms, not cause; they are pruning branches, not digging up the root. The ultimate issue behind poverty is sin.

Having said that, however, we need to go even deeper. We need to introduce the core idea of the rest of this book.

In the final analysis, sin is *the* poverty from which we *all* suffer.

The Ultimate Poverty

Let me be clear. I am not saying that material poverty comes when God punishes particular individuals or particular people for particular sins. At times, God may choose to discipline people through material means, but a "punishment" view of poverty is not necessary to account for the poverty we see. We live in a fallen world, a world living under a curse as the direct result of Adam and Eve's sin, and that in itself is more than enough to account for the world's poverty.

The first man and woman were created in the image and likeness of God and declared "very good" in his eyes. They were then given the task of serving as God's representatives within creation. For a time, they lived in perfect harmony with God, each other, and the world around them. But when they chose to sin, everything changed. Their original identity was lost. Their relationships with God, with each other, and with the world were broken, devastated, ruined.

This is poverty in its most true and ultimate sense. Incomparable riches—an unbroken relationship with God and a harmonious relationship with the rest of creation—have been squandered. Everything about our existence has been impoverished as a result of sin.

A fallen world inhabited exclusively by sinners: that is the essence of poverty. Sin, and the effects of sin throughout creation, is the Poverty from which all other poverty flows.

As we will see in the next chapter, this reality should have profound implications for how we understand, think about, and respond to material poverty.

Reflect, Discuss, Apply

1. Read Genesis 1:1-2:3. Why does God look at his work and declare it good? Why is this important?
2. What was the only thing God said was "not good"?
3. What was mankind's role within creation? What does it mean to "subdue the earth and have dominion"?
4. Read Genesis 3:1-19. What impact did the Fall have on Adam and Eve's relationship with God, each other, and the world?
5. How does that affect your understanding of poverty?

Two

WHOSE KINGDOM?

The Lure of Utopian Dreams

Growing up, one of my favorite movies was *The Goonies*. It has everything a boy could ask for—adventure, humor, action, and only a little of the mushy stuff. The plot is a classic: after finding a treasure map in his attic, Mikey and his friends go on a wild adventure in search of the hidden fortune of the infamous pirate One-Eyed Willy. As they travel through an underground maze full of dangers and skeletons, they become trapped at the bottom of the town's wishing well. Faced with the choice of going forward or riding the water bucket back to the surface, Mikey pleads with them to persevere:

> Don't you realize? The next time you see sky, it'll be over another town. The next time you take a test, it'll be in some other school. Our parents, they want the best of stuff for us. But right now, they got to do what's right for them. Because it's their time. Their time! Up there! Down here, it's *our* time. *It's our*

time down here. That's all over the second we ride up Troy's bucket.[27]

The scene still gets to me. I think it must be Mikey's desire for significance. He wants to do something memorable, something important. I can relate.

Many of us want to be more than we are. It's as if we know there's something missing in our lives, and we're willing to do almost anything to get it. We want to be remembered as someone who was important, who made a positive difference in the world. We want to have a legacy.

The Bible is full of stories about people out to do remarkable things. Some want to glorify God, while others only want to glorify themselves. One thing we see time and time again: sin keeps getting in the way.

Adam's Legacy: Sin and Death

After Adam and Eve were driven from the garden, they started having babies. When her son Cain was born, Eve rejoiced, saying, "I have gotten a man with the help of the Lord."[28] Cain offered the banished first family a glimmer of hope, for God's curse upon Adam, Eve, and the serpent had been accompanied by a promise—the seed of the woman would crush the seed of the serpent.[29] Eve may well have imagined that the curse would be broken through Cain. Then they could all return to the Garden, their relationship with God restored. But if Adam and Eve held any hope of this happening through Cain, that hope was dashed when Cain murdered his brother Abel and was condemned to wander the earth.[30]

This was Adam's legacy — death. Not only was his firstborn son a murderer, not only was Abel dead, but Adam's sons and grandsons yet follow him into death. Adam, Seth, Enosh, Kenan, Mahalalel, Jared, Methuselah, Lamech . . . as we read through Adam's lineage, everyone but Enoch[31] receives the same understated eulogy: "And he died."[32] They were born, had children, and died. That's virtually everything the Bible says about them, a painful reminder of the deadly consequences of sin.

Death is a foreign element in creation. It repels us. No matter how much we try to convince ourselves otherwise, we know deep down that something as awful as death was never meant to be the conclusion to something as wonderful as life. But Adam and Eve's ambitious and fateful rebellion added sin and death into the DNA of creation, beginning an inevitable slide into disaster.

Not too many generations after Cain killed Abel, God rendered the following judgment:

> The Lord saw that the wickedness of man was great in the earth, and that every intention of the thoughts of his heart was only evil continually. And the Lord was sorry that he had made man on the earth, and it grieved him to his heart. So the Lord said, "I will blot out man whom I have created from the face of the land, man and animals and creeping things and birds of the heavens, for I am sorry that I have made them."[33]

Mankind had slid so far into the depths of depravity that *every* thought motive on the face of the earth had become evil. God responded to this sin in righteous judgment by sending the Flood: everything and everyone would die. All had been found guilty; all were condemned.

All but Noah, who had "found favor in the eyes of the Lord."[34] Although Noah and his family also deserved judgment, in mercy God chose to save them. He began by instructing Noah to build the ark, and Noah obeyed, constructing an ark that would preserve his family and two of every kind of animal on the earth.[35] The rains came, covering the face of the earth and killing everyone and everything that had not found shelter on the ark. After God's judgment was complete, Noah and his family left the ark and offered a sacrifice to the Lord[36], who responded,

> I will never again curse the ground because of man, for the intention of man's heart is evil from his youth. Neither will I ever again strike down every living creature as I have done. While the earth remains, seedtime and harvest, cold and heat, summer and winter, day and night, shall not cease.[37]

If there were ever a chance for perfection to return, this would have been the moment. Yet, despite this great purging of sin over the entire face of the earth, God still says, "the intention of man's heart is evil from his youth." Why? Because man is still fallen; the curse is still in effect.

Sin is not an environmental condition or something that varies in its essence from one person to another. It's a universal heart issue. Not *caused* by circumstances, sin is *resident* in the heart of man, who innately loves evil and the "works of darkness."[38] As much hope as there is in the birth of Cain, because he is part of the promised offspring that will eventually crush evil, death and destruction also follow him and his descendants. Adam's legacy is unchanged.

On the Building of Towers

People seem to be wired to want to do something significant, to reach for accomplishment, to establish a legacy, whether great or small. Yet we live in a world that is cursed, and sin tends to turn everything wrong. Let's consider two examples relating to poverty.

The Great Recession took hold globally in 2008, with the most obvious measurable impacts beginning in the North American housing market. The first wave of the recession devastated thousands of peoples' retirement savings, bankrupted thousands more, and pushed roughly 64 million into extreme poverty.[39] What caused it? Sin. Sinful greed allowed sub-prime mortgages to spin out of control as people borrowed more money than they could ever hope to repay. A deadly combination of covetousness and foolishness allowed North Americans to develop a massive level of consumer debt that they often serviced with home equity loans. It was "the desires of the flesh and the desires of the eyes and pride in possessions"[40] run amok. And a whole lot of people's lives were ruined or seriously thrown off track when they became trapped in the middle of it.

Consider, too, an irony that has developed in international giving during the past 40-plus years. In this time, the world's richest nations have given unprecedented amounts of aid to poorer countries. As a result, some amazing things have happened. Millions of children are alive today who would otherwise have died by age 5. Fewer children are dying of preventable illnesses like malaria and diarrhea. And fewer people in general are living in what would be considered extreme poverty.[41]

Yet Sub-Saharan Africa continues to languish in horrific poverty. Why? Because of sin; corrupt officials routinely siphon off aid money in the affected countries. So while aid can be helpful, we can never completely remove the human factor from our efforts, and we must remember that "the intention of man's heart is evil from his youth." Some people even aim opportunistically to profit at the expense of others. It was true when Cain killed Abel, it was true when Noah and his family boarded the ark, and it was still true when they got off the ark. Sure enough, it wasn't long after the earth dried out before sin renewed its reign over creation, this time in the form of people trying to impress others with a massive building project.

Noah's descendants multiplied and filled the earth, and all "had one language and the same words."[42] United in language and in commitment to sin, mankind decided to build themselves a city, "and a tower with its top in the heavens." And they said, "let us make a name for ourselves, lest we be dispersed over the face of the whole earth."[43]

As I read those words, they remind me of other statements with a strikingly similar self-promoting tone:

- Mikey's speech from *The Goonies*: "It's [our parents'] time . . . up there! Down here, it's *our* time. *It's our time down here.*"

- The St. Crispin's Day speech from Shakespeare's *Henry V*, before the Battle of Agincourt: "This story shall the good man teach his son; / And Crispin Crispian shall ne'er go by, / From this day to the ending of the world, / But we in it shall be remembered— / We few, we happy few, we band of brothers" (IV.iii.56-60).
- Words from a recent presidential campaign seeking to inspire a nation with hope for a better tomorrow:
- We have been told we cannot do this by a chorus of cynics. . . . We've been asked to pause for a reality check. We've been warned against offering the people of this nation false hope. . . . [When] we've been told we're not ready or that we shouldn't try or that we can't, generations of Americans have responded with a simple creed that sums up the spirit of a people: "Yes, we can." . . . Yes, we can, to justice and equality. Yes, we can, to opportunity and prosperity. Yes, we can heal this nation. Yes, we can repair this world. Yes, we can.[44]

A similar attitude is prevalent in the antipoverty community. In fact, among those hundreds or thousands of organizations dedicated to serving the poor, one familiar-sounding declaration tends to summarize their shared mission: *"We can we end world poverty."*

It is not always worded quite this way, not always overtly emphasized, but it is almost always there. This sentiment captures the primary motivating force behind nearly the entire antipoverty movement.

It sounds noble and wonderful, and the motivations behind it are not entirely bad. But unless you believe the Bible's testimony about the pervasive nature of sin, this statement can introduce serious problems and real danger. Man-made efforts at man-made salvation never end well.

At the risk of oversimplifying, there are two kinds of people in the anti-poverty movement: 1) those who *do not* understand and acknowledge the pervasive, persistent role of sin and the fall in inclining man to poverty, and 2) those who do understand.

Those who don't. Those who do not understand are fighting blind. They may have valuable skills, great resources, and deep understanding in many pertinent areas. But because they cannot even see the main enemy, their efforts are compromised before they begin.

Those who do. Many of those who do understand poverty's connection to sin have the same level of skills, resources, and understanding as those who do not. While their ability to recognize the role of sin and the fall in poverty does not in itself guarantee they will be more effective, it does allow them to more comprehensively care for the needs of those suffering in its midst.

Regardless, the issue before God is not whether you understand the essential challenges underlying poverty. The issue is your heart motivation for pursuing its eradication.

Why Do We Build?

"Let us make a name for ourselves," the people said as they erected the Tower of Babel. And so they still say today — even if they don't realize it. Many well-meaning, sincere people (including some Christian leaders) have bought into the desire to "make a name for ourselves," even with such a noble goal as ending poverty. "We are the generation that can end poverty," they say. "This is our time; this can be our legacy. We can make a dramatic impact in the fight against poverty."

My concern is not that people are calling attention to the plight of the global poor. If anything, we may need to be reminded more often, not less. My concern, and even my fear, is whether we have gotten off-track and become more concerned with our own legacies and our own kingdoms than with Christ's. We may have developed a god-complex. Steve Corbett and Brian Fikkert describe this as a "subtle and unconscious sense of superiority in which [the economically rich] believe that they have achieved their wealth through their own efforts and that they have been anointed to decide what is best for low income people, whom they view as inferior to themselves."[45]

And what makes this so devastating is that few of us are even *aware* that we have this problem! "We are often deceived by Satan and by our sinful natures," Corbett and Fikkert explain, echoing the Apostle Paul, who wrote, "when I want to do right, evil lies close at hand."[46] Thus, our need for discernment cannot be overstated. We must carefully and prayerfully examine our hearts and motives when considering our approach to caring for the poor.

When the people of Babel agreed together to build a tower with its top in the heavens, they wanted to make a name for themselves. They wanted to be known, honored, and glorified on their own merit for building a tower at

33

which others would have to stop and marvel. But what
was God's response? Did he commend their ingenuity?
Did he admire their ambition?

> And the Lord came down to see the city and the
> tower, which the children of man had built. And the
> Lord said, "Behold, they are one people, and they
> have all one language, and this is only the beginning of
> what they will do. And nothing that they propose to
> do will now be impossible for them. Come, let us go
> down and there confuse their language, so that they
> may not understand one another's speech."[47]

Rather than look on their work with pleasure, God
looked on it with great concern. Kent Hughes explains why:

> The problem with the tower as such lay . . . in its
> underlying suppositions and approach. . . . The
> unadorned belief that man by his superior effort
> could reach God betrays the fatal delusion of all
> man-made religion. This delusion is at the heart
> of every religious enterprise apart from the gospel
> because the world's religions all teach that works
> bring spiritual advance — as in an improved karma
> or works-righteousness. Collective apostasy had
> engulfed the descendants of Shem, Ham, and Japheth
> as they stacked their bricks up to heaven.[48]

When we consider Christian responses to the needs of
the poor, Hughes' explanation should give us pause. We

may be too humble to proclaim our own glory, but few of us are humble enough not to hope for it, and to quietly smile when our good works are noticed. Kindness—even kindness done in line with God's commands—can be motivated by a self-glorifying heart.

Unity as Apostasy

The current discussion about poverty has a common theme: most people who think poverty can be eliminated also think humanity must be united to achieve it. If we are one in purpose, the thinking goes, nothing can stop us from achieving our goal:

- All 191 UN member states unanimously agreed to the Millennium Development Goals. The first of those goals is to eradicate extreme poverty.[49]
- Jeffrey Sachs believes that if we are united in purpose and tactics, we can end extreme poverty by 2025.[50]
- Paul Collier believes the eight richest nations of the world need to be united in creating new laws and charters designed to assist reformers within the 50 poorest countries in their quest to change their countries for the better, and that the rest of us need to unite in pressuring them to do so.[51]

There's nothing inherently wrong with any of these options. Building a tower *can* be a morally neutral endeavor. But it comes back to the "why." Are we seeking somehow to make a name for *ourselves*, or are we seeking to make much of God's name?

The tower builders in Genesis 11 knew exactly whose reputation they were seeking to erect. But instead of being exalted, they became associated with one of the most overt acts of pride in human history. "Their name would become a joke," writes Hughes. "The tower builders were a broken people. And the fact that they feared being scattered is proof that their fellowship with God and their unity with each other had been shattered by sin."[52] Together, they would only have continued to work for the magnification of their own sinful nature. So God, in his mercy, did exactly what they feared. Rather than allow them to remain united in sin and folly, God confused their languages and "dispersed them over the face of all the earth."[53]

Sometimes I wonder if that "confusion of languages" dynamic is not still at work, a means by which God hinders our ongoing attempts at uniting this fallen race for the sake of our own glorification. Anyone who pays attention to politics recognizes that people in the same society can have radically different views of reality. For example, people on the political left typically hold a distinctly different perspective on the nature of man than that of people on the political right, leading to distinctly different views on a great many issues. Because they see the world differently, the two groups can weigh the same evidence and draw different conclusions. In many ways, they don't speak the same language or think the same way.

Something similar happens among those in the antipoverty movement. Consider all the disagreement on how best to alleviate poverty. Where some believe it's ultimately about increasing foreign aid, others believe it's about the right combination of legislation and economic opportunity. Where some believe sending workers from rich nations to build houses, hospitals, and schools is a wonderful way to help, others believe it ultimately robs the poor of opportunities to help themselves. Why can we not agree on the best way to pursue a resolution to this situation? Why do some "reject the plaintive cries of the doomsayers who say that ending poverty is impossible," and not engage in honest dialogue?[54] Why do some see the nearly consistent failure of aid money to make an impact in Africa and altogether give up trying to do anything?

It's a little like after Babel, isn't it? You say one thing, but I may hear something else. We talk past each other. We see the world differently and therefore come to different conclusions based on the same evidence. Why?

Is it possible that our motives are not nearly as altruistic as they may appear? Is it possible that our desire for significance, to leave a legacy and be known as the generation that eradicated extreme global poverty, is actually preventing us from getting much closer to doing it? Do we have a God-complex?

In a sense, God *has* confused our language, for he has no interest in a vast unity of man that is self-focused, self-congratulatory, and self-worshiping. He alone is God.

When Adam and Eve sinned, it was because they wanted to be like God. As humanity multiplied and filled the earth, sin multiplied with them. Our desire for significance, twisted by sin, always drives us to rob God of his glory and make a name for ourselves instead. This pursuit will always fail, and quite often we will do substantial harm to our fellow man in the process. God will share his glory with no one, and he will thwart any attempt designed to make a name for ourselves. Whether working on a tower whose top is intended to reach the heavens, or deciding we can end poverty by 2025 — if our motive is anything other than making God's name great, the effort will be divinely dismantled.

At the same time, we *are* called to care for the poor, and we *can* do this to the glory of God. What does that look like? We'll begin to examine that question in the next chapter.

Reflect, Discuss, Apply

1. Why do you want to help the poor? What truly motivates you to do this?

2. In your own words, what does the author mean by a "god-complex"? If you suffer from this, how does it manifest itself? How can you put it to death in your life?

3. Read Genesis 6-9. What is significant about the account of the global flood? Why did God send it? Why does God say afterwards, "the intention of man's heart is evil from his youth"?

4. Read Genesis 11. What implication does this chapter carry for us today?

5. The author writes that "God will share his glory with no one, and he will thwart any attempt designed to make a name for ourselves." Do you agree? How should this affect our attitude toward ideas such as eliminating global poverty?

Three
LIGHT TO THE NATIONS?

God's Covenant and the State of Our Hearts

One of the best days of my life was when Emily and I got married. About 50 people attended the ceremony and reception, and the weather was excellent. After the beautiful, simple service we kicked back and enjoyed quirky music, fellowship, and good food. Emily was stunning the entire time. But of all the joyful moments of the day, one thing stands out: our vows. As we spoke them, Emily and I entered into a covenant with each other before God, agreeing to love, encourage, serve, and support one another until death do us part.

These vows we did not make lightly. We knew there would be challenges, so before either of us said, "I do," we had to decide if we were really in it to win it. Was I really up for loving Emily as Christ loves the Church? Was Emily really up for helping and encouraging me to take the lead in our family? Did we both mean it when we agreed that the only thing that would end our marriage would be death?

Marriage presents a unique opportunity to display God's glory, and the only way to take advantage of that particular opportunity is to enter into a solemn, binding, lifelong agreement. We knew that, and we wanted that, so that's what we did. Before God and all those witnesses, Emily and I joined together in a covenant.

Throughout Scripture, indeed from the opening chapters of Genesis, we see that God is one who makes covenants. Beginning with Adam, he entered into a covenantal relationship with humanity. He renewed that covenant with Noah and, later, expanded it with Abraham. With Moses and the nation of Israel, Abraham's descendants, God also formed a covenant.[55] Made first at Sinai and renewed prior to the nation's crossing into the Promised Land, the Mosaic covenant gave explicit instructions for how the Israelites are to live as God's redeemed people. It contains 613 laws—248 positive and 365 negative—covering the moral, social, and ceremonial realms. No area of life was untouched by the Law.[56]

Why did God feel the need to be so intimately involved with every detail of the Israelites' life? Why did he tell them, "These are the things you may eat, the clothes you shall wear, and the days you may work?" Theologians have settled on two basic reasons: 1) Israel was to be *set apart*, and 2) Israel was to be set apart *for a purpose*.

Set apart. God had the right to mandate how the Israelites were to live *because they belonged to him*. "The Lord has brought you out with a mighty hand and redeemed you from the house of slavery, from the hand of Pharaoh king of Egypt."[57] Therefore, they were commanded to "be careful to do the commandment and the statutes and the rules" that God gave them specifically.[58] They were to be a holy people, set apart from all the other nations. Why?

For a purpose. Israel was to be set apart *from* the nations that they might be a light *to* the nations, a light making known the glory and greatness of God.[59] In all things and in all ways the Israelites were to be different—including in their treatment of the poor.

No Poor Among You

The book of Deuteronomy contains Moses' re-presentation of the Law to the Israelites as they were preparing to enter the Promised Land. Chapter 15 involves God's intentions for the sabbatical year and how his people are to respond to the needs of the poor among them.

The sabbatical year worked like this: at the end of every seven years, all debts would be forgiven, all the economic slates wiped clean. It didn't matter if a loan was given in the first, second, or sixth year. At the end of the seventh, the reset button was pushed and life went on.[60] These sabbatical year commands, and indeed the Mosaic Law as it pertains to economics, were all about a spirit of generosity. And so we come to this bold statement:

> *There will be no poor among you*; for the LORD will bless you in the land that the LORD your God is giving you for an inheritance to possess—if only you will strictly obey the voice of the LORD your God, being

careful to do all this commandment that I command
you today. For the LORD your God will bless you, as
he promised you, and you shall lend to many nations,
but you shall not borrow, and you shall rule over
many nations, but they shall not rule over you.[61]

We need to recognize that this is a promise with a
contingency. The passage specifies that *if* the Israelites
obey God's laws, including the economic ones, *then*
they would see great material blessing and the needs of all
would thus be met; there would be *no poor among them*.
In other words, God says that his covenant blessings are
contingent on the Israelites' covenant faithfulness. They
would prosper *only* if they were faithful to his commands.
Yet the very next passage seems to acknowledge that this
will not happen:

> *If among you, one of your brothers should become*
> *poor* . . . you shall not harden your heart or shut your
> hand against your poor brother, but you shall open
> your hand to him and lend him sufficient for his need,
> whatever it may be. . . . *For there will never cease to*
> *be poor in the land.* Therefore I command you, "You
> shall open wide your hand to your brother, to the
> needy and to the poor, in your land."[62]

God essentially says to the Israelites, "There will be
no poor among you as long as you fully obey my laws.
But I know what is in the heart of man, that his every
thought is always evil continually, so let me warn you

right now — there will never cease to be some among you who are poor."

God knew that sin still reigned in the hearts of the Israelites. Though they had been freed from bondage to Egypt, they were still in bondage to sin. They were not righteous but "a stubborn people."[63] While Deuteronomy 15 promised them blessing and encouraged generosity, it also warned against the failure of generosity. It warned against a hardness of heart toward the poor:

> Take care lest there be an unworthy thought in your heart and you say, "The seventh year, the year of release is near," and your eye look grudgingly on your poor brother, and you give him nothing, and he cry to the LORD against you, and you be guilty of sin. You shall give to him freely, and your heart shall not be grudging when you give to him, because for this the LORD your God will bless you in all your work and in all that you undertake.[64]

How often have we heard or spoken grudging words? "The reason they're poor is they don't work hard. If they just tried a little harder, they wouldn't be in the mess they're in." Or "I'm not going to give him any money. He's probably going to just spend it on booze." Or "They made their bed, let them lie in it."

Why do we do this? Why do we look at others and their circumstances and declare them worthy or unworthy of our assistance?

A Covenant of Compassion

As we consider that question, we must note that the Law drew a distinction between God's people and the surrounding nations, even in matters of economic compassion. The passages above, for example, speak only about caring for poor *Israelites*. Elsewhere, the Israelites were forbidden from charging *one another* interest, yet no such restriction existed when dealing with the foreigner.[65] God's expectations for interactions between Israelites are entirely different. There is a higher priority placed on mutual care and compassion.

This does not mean, however, that those outside the covenant community could be conveniently ignored— only that concern and care for those within the covenant community takes precedence. (It is the same way today within the Church.) Indeed, the Law included a radical concern for the "sojourner," the foreigner among them,[66] a concern that stems directly from the heart of God: "For the LORD your God is God of gods and Lord of lords, the great, the mighty, and the awesome God, who is not partial . . . and *loves the sojourner*, giving him food and clothing. Love the sojourner, therefore, for you were in the land of Egypt."[67]

God loves the "sojourner," and God's people are to love him as well. That's why, although we must be wise in how we help those in need,[68] we must avoid notions of anyone being "deserving" of our help. None of us deserve the grace of God, yet he freely gives it!

The Israelites were freed from slavery because the Lord loved them and kept the oath that he swore to

Abraham, Isaac, and Jacob. When he gave them the Promised Land, it was not because of their righteousness, for they were a stubborn people. In the wilderness, they provoked him to anger, worshiping the golden calf, grumbling and complaining endlessly. If a people were ever completely *un*deserving of God's mercy, it was the Israelites! Yet, God *still* brought them to the land he had promised.[69]

Is this any less true of us? How can we, if we have been saved through Christ, say to anyone, "You are not worthy of my help"? How we help may vary from situation to situation (something that we'll look at in later chapters), but no one should be considered unworthy of assistance.

Look again at Deuteronomy 15:9, where God warns the Israelites to "take care lest there be an unworthy thought in your heart." This exhortation to "take care" is repeated nine times in Deuteronomy.[70] Each time it points to the Israelites' inclination to forget what God had done for them and the heart's desire to rebel against him and chase after idols. So God warns them, over and over again: "Take care, lest your heart be drawn away.... Take care lest you forget all that I've done in your midst.... Take care lest you forget to obey all I have commanded you." Yet, despite these warnings, despite the repeated promises of blessing and the warning of curses, the Israelites repeatedly failed to keep God's commands. They did not—*they could not*—remain faithful to his covenant. Their hearts were bad. And that ruined everything.

The Problem of Sin

The Israelites of old were not alone in this. A bad heart—
an "uncircumcised heart," a heart drawn away from the
worship of God to the worship of anything but God—is
the fundamental problem of the human race[71] and indeed
the fundamental problem of poverty. This is the heart of
sin.

Sin has marred our identity as God's image bearers
and crippled our relationship with God, one another, and
the world around us. Sin thus not only *causes* poverty but
also poisons our attitude toward those suffering within it.

To summarize some key points from this book so far,
poverty stems from the fall in at least three ways:

- God's curse upon Adam's economic labors makes
  prosperity difficult and elusive.
- We rebel against God, and he withholds material
  blessing in response, that we might be drawn back to
  him when our idols fail us.
- We neglect our God-ordained duty of generosity to
  one another, a duty to provide material goods and
  economic opportunities to the less fortunate among
  us.

Better-focused anti-poverty campaigns and the
implementation of superior development strategies are
important. But these cannot begin to touch the root, the
underlying cause of poverty. Ultimately, poverty can only
be addressed at the heart level, one person at a time, as
salvation through the shed blood of Christ pushes back

against the fall of man. The ultimate answer to poverty is circumcised hearts, hearts that know the God who forms and keeps covenant with poor, undeserving sinners.

Reflect, Discuss, Apply

1. What does it mean to be in a covenant? Why does it matter that God makes covenants with people?
2. Read Deuteronomy 15:1-11. What was God's intention for the Israelites in giving these laws surrounding the sabbatical year?
3. Why does God warn against hard-hearted attitudes surrounding generosity? Have you ever tried to justify helping or not helping the poor with a statement like the examples above? Why? Do you think that attitude derives more from biblical teaching or from ideas based in politics?

Four
FAITH WITH WORKS

The Evidence of a Changed Heart

As Moses began to approach the end of his life, it didn't take a prophet to see that the Israelites would still *need* a prophet—someone sent by God to call them back when they went astray. So Moses, expressing to the people God's unfailing mercy and compassion, promised Israel that God would continue to send prophets.[72] And of course, God did send prophets, although not immediately.

After the death of Moses' successor Joshua, the people, as if on cue, slipped into idolatry. By the end of the period of the Judges, the nation, settled in the Promised Land, had fully embraced depravity: "Everyone did what was right in his own eyes."[73] Their pursuits were for selfish gain, not God's glory. They desired to make much of themselves, not the one who had rescued them out of bondage in Egypt. The Israelites' uncircumcised hearts wandered after idols. Even Solomon, the wisest man ever to live, began worshipping the gods of his many wives and concubines, and the nation followed his example.

Jeroboam, becoming king over the northern part of the land, set up for himself two golden calves and commanded the worship and service of these idols rather than the true God whose temple resided in Jerusalem to the south.[74] What followed was a succession of rulers of whom it was said — 24 times in the books of 1 and 2 Kings alone — he "did what was evil in the sight of the Lord."[75]

And so the prophets came to the children of Israel. This was not the first appearance of a prophet since the time of Moses. Nathan, for example, had earlier spoken to David of his sin with Bathsheba. But now, God began to send prophets to speak to the entire nation, with their words and deeds recorded in Scripture at length.

The Message of Repentance

The prophets of Israel spoke with a single voice; their message to the people was to repent. "Repent and turn away from your idols, and turn away your faces from all your abominations," these prophets said. "Repent and turn from all your transgressions, lest iniquity be your ruin."[76] Every word they spoke was to call the wandering heart of Israel back to the Lord. Israel's idolatry had left them a corrupt people, spiritually bankrupt, "lovers of pleasure rather than lovers of God."[77]

What evidence does Scripture offer that the people were spiritually bankrupt? That they failed to seek justice for the oppressed. And just so we are clear what God means by "justice" and "the oppressed," he specifies — as we will see in a few paragraphs — what he is talking about: the plight of the hungry, the homeless, and the ill-clothed.

Isaiah. Isaiah 58 offers one of the harshest rebukes of sinful complacency, lambasting the outwardly pious but inwardly corrupt Israelites. "They seek me daily and delight to know my ways, as if they were a nation that did righteousness and did not forsake the judgment of their God," we read in Isaiah 58:2.

Though the Israelites outwardly appeared to delight in God, they turned to him and asked, with more than a hint of offense, "*Why* have we fasted, and you see it not? *Why* have we humbled ourselves, and you take no knowledge of it?"[78] They were deeply offended that despite their external performance—after all, they prayed, they fasted, they tithed, they kept the feasts that God had appointed—God failed to shower them with blessing. "Is our worship not good enough for you?" they asked.

How did God respond? Was he convinced by their appeal? Did he receive it well? Did he say, "Oh, sorry about that; I've been really busy and didn't notice. Great work, keep it up"? No. He called their bluff and challenged their so-called piety:

> Behold, in the day of your fast you seek your own pleasure, and oppress all your workers. Behold, you fast only to quarrel and to fight and to hit with a wicked fist. Fasting like yours this day will not make your voice to be heard on high.

> Is such the fast that I choose, a day for a person to humble himself? Is it to bow down his head like a reed, and to spread sackcloth and ashes under him?

> Will you call this a fast, and a day acceptable to the
> LORD?[79]

Their "worship" was only intended to be seen by
others; it came not from a desire to truly please God, nor
from a heart that longed to know him deeply. Their desire,
God said, was to "seek [their] own pleasure . . . to quarrel
and to fight and to hit with a wicked fist."

"What to me is the multitude of your sacrifices?" God
asked in an earlier discourse. "I have had enough of burnt
offerings and . . . do not delight in the blood of bulls, or of
lambs, or of goats." God hated the Israelites' feasts and
assemblies. He tired of their offerings. He ignored their
prayers.[80] The Israelites were trying to use the system
of worship that God had established to manipulate him,
all the while ignoring their responsibilities toward him.
They loved their sin, and the Lord did not listen to their
prayers.[81] Their worship was not acceptable.

But what did God say *was* acceptable? If their fasting
and prayers, their outward obedience to the ceremonial
laws, was not valid evidence of worship to God, what was?

> Is not this the fast that I choose: to loose the bonds of
> wickedness, to undo the straps of the yoke, to let the
> oppressed go free, and to break every yoke?
>
> Is it not to share your bread with *the hungry* and
> bring *the homeless poor* into your house; when you
> see *the naked*, to cover him, and not to hide yourself
> from your own flesh?[82]

Amos, Jeremiah, Ezekiel. Isaiah was not alone in making the connection between holiness and acts of genuine compassion. Amos offered a stinging rebuke to many in Israel's northern kingdom, whose extravagant and self-indulgent lifestyles were built on the oppression of the poor and perverse idol worship.[83] Jeremiah also decried their sin, saying, "on your skirts is found the lifeblood of the guiltless poor; you did not find them breaking in. Yet ... you say, 'I am innocent.'"[84]

Ezekiel warned the prideful people of Jerusalem, who oppressed the poor and needy, that they would face the same judgment as Sodom.[85] Can you imagine that? Sodom was one of the most evil, despicable cities ever on the face of the earth, where a gang came to Lot's door and demanded he send out his male guests so they could rape them in the street.[86] You wouldn't expect this kind of comparison, yet here it is. God tells his people that when they oppress the poor and needy, they are as bad as the men of Sodom.

The Fruit of Repentance

Disgusted by the Israelites' false worship, God spoke repeatedly through his prophets: "You say you worship me; you say you are right in my sight, yet your lives reveal you to be liars!" But God's rebukes were joined by another message, a message of hope and reconciliation and cleansing.

If the people would repent and turn to God, he would hear them and turn from his anger. And perhaps surprisingly, God emphasizes that this change of heart in

the people would be reflected in a change of behavior—
their repentance would bring about a revival of justice.
The Israelites' change of heart toward God would be
evidenced, in no small part, by a change of heart and
action toward the poor and oppressed:

> Wash yourselves; make yourselves clean; remove the
> evil of your deeds from before my eyes; cease to do
> evil, learn to do good; seek justice, correct oppres-
> sion; bring justice to the fatherless, plead the widow's
> cause....
> If you take away the yoke from your midst, the
> pointing of the finger, and speaking wickedness, if
> you pour yourself out for the hungry and satisfy the
> desire of the afflicted, then shall your light rise in the
> darkness and your gloom be as the noonday.[87]
>
> ....
>
> Take away from me the noise of your songs; to the
> melody of your harps I will not listen. But let justice
> roll down like waters, and righteousness like an ever-
> flowing stream.[88]

It might seem strange to see the word "justice" used
in connection with caring for the poor. After all, this word
tends to function a bit fluidly in our culture. Different people
use it in various ways. For some, it's an issue of equality, pro-
tecting the rights of one person from being infringed upon
by another. For others, it's a matter of retribution, ensuring
that those who commit a crime are prosecuted. These are
right and true and biblical as far as they go.

But "justice" carries a deeper meaning in Scripture than our culture allows. That's because justice is grounded in and stems from the character of God himself. As Wayne Grudem puts it so succinctly, "whatever conforms to God's moral character is right," or *just*[89] because "*all* his ways are justice . . . *just* and *upright* is he."[90] In whatever God does and declares, he is both just and righteous because he is just and righteous by his very nature.

So what has he declared to be just? Is it not to "pour yourself out for the hungry and satisfy the desire of the afflicted"? Is it not to "correct oppression"? Is it not to obey him in all that he commands — especially in caring for the poor and needy among us?

That's what it means to be faithful to God's covenant, and (as we saw in the previous chapter), that's exactly what the Israelites were incapable of doing. It's what Samuel meant when he said to King Saul, "Has the LORD as great delight in burnt offerings and sacrifices, as in obeying the voice of the LORD? Behold, to obey is better than sacrifice, and to listen than the fat of rams."[91] It's what Jesus meant when he told the disciples, "If you love me, you will keep my commandments."[92]

Covenant faithfulness is obedience — obedience motivated not out of obligation or duty or a desire to score points with God but out of love for God.

As we try to obey God in all areas of our lives — how we use our time, money, and talents — there is not a single aspect of life that is not affected, including how we relate to others. Jesus told his disciples that the greatest commandments of all are to "love the Lord your God with all your heart and with all your soul and with all your might" and to "love your neighbor as yourself" because "On these two commandments depend all the Law and the Prophets."[93] If you separate the second of those commands from the first, *you fail to obey either one*. The Bible could not be more clear about this.

Loving our neighbor in real, tangible ways is as much a "proof" of our salvation as anything else. How we relate to God directly affects how we relate to others. Unfaithfulness to the Lord *will* lead to a lack of concern for our neighbor—but the opposite should also be true.

And who is our neighbor? The parable of the Good Samaritan[94] answers plainly. Someone who has a genuine need, a need we become aware of, and a need we are able to meet, even if it results in inconvenience to ourselves—this person is our neighbor.

Ethical Faithfulness Is Covenant Faithfulness

Ray Ortlund's take on the connection between revival of the soul and a renewed sense of justice is helpful. "True revival isn't a private religious joyride," he writes. "It gets us busy, doing what we can about poverty, illiteracy, slavery, abortion, political manipulation, people being treated like animals, people going to eternal Hell."[95]

Those whose hearts are inclined to the Lord will seek true justice on earth as it is in heaven. *Covenant faithfulness always leads to ethical faithfulness.*[96] The faithful will seek to care for the poor around them, to "share [their] bread with the hungry, to cover the naked, and to "let the oppressed go free." They will "bear fruit in keeping with repentance."[97] They will pursue justice in the full biblical sense of the term.

Is it any wonder, then, that the words of Isaiah have become a clarion call for so many Christians who are concerned about the welfare of the world's poor? They are right to take up this cause. The need is vast. In Africa, children still die every day from malaria because they can't afford a $15 bed net. In Haiti, homes, schools, hospitals, and churches still lie in ruins years after the January 2010 earthquake.

The problem is in North America, too. In the United States, approximately 15.4 million Americans live in extreme poverty.[98] This is not a matter of being unable to afford an Xbox—they can't afford to eat. Isaiah's words offer strong medicine to those of us who risk becoming complacent or even apathetic toward the poor and oppressed of this world. We dare not turn a blind eye. We dare not think, "They're somebody else's problem." If we really mean that, our hearts are as dead as those of the unfaithful Israelites of Isaiah's day.

Don't Ask the Wrong Question

I am not suggesting that the answers to these dilemmas are necessarily simple, for this world is still fallen and people are still sinners. My point is that the need exists, and covenant faithfulness demands we not simply ignore it. So when I read the dire warnings of the prophets— when I look at the reality that covenant faithfulness leads to ethical faithfulness—I inevitably ask, "Am I doing enough?" But as I've continued to study Isaiah, I'm not sure this is the right question. In fact, it might be exactly the *wrong* one.

"Doing enough" can be overly simplistic. One problem with "doing enough" is that it tends to focus us on the wrong goal. We pick a dollar amount, or an income percentage, or a number of hours per month. We construct a set of checkboxes to see if we're meeting the output criteria we have set for ourselves. Some suggest, for example, that if we all give just *one percent* more financially, global poverty can be wiped out forever. All we have to do, they say, is track the progress, allocate the resources, and we're set.

When "doing enough" becomes primarily a matter of numbers, we can be sure we are focusing on the wrong thing. Alleviating poverty is about more than a certain amount of giving, whether of time or money. (More on this in future chapters.)

"Doing enough" is legalism. Worse, this "doing enough" mindset is textbook legalism—the effort to be pleasing to God through our external behavior. And *encouraging* people to be active in helping the poor can promote legalism like few other activities. Unless God cuts someone to the heart and instills a compassion for the poor, exhortations to "choose your fast" or "just give more money" either will be ignored or will feed one's "inner legalist."

If our focus is whether we are doing "enough," it may be that our hearts are as dead as those to whom Isaiah,

Amos, Jeremiah, and Ezekiel preached. "We have all become like one who is unclean," Isaiah said, "and all our righteous deeds are like a polluted garment."[99]

This shocking simile confronts us with the reality that it's not only our sins that are offensive, but "our *righteousness* stinks."[100] There is nothing that we can do *on our own* to please God. Outward ceremony doesn't please him and neither do "righteous" deeds. False piety of any kind is disgusting to him.

This takes us back to our fundamental need for a circumcised heart. If we expect to end poverty, we need to deal with our sin problem first. To deal with our sin problem, we need a heart that's inclined toward the Lord. And this heart is something only God can give us. Fortunately, he promises to do exactly that:

> Behold, the days are coming, declares the LORD, when I will make a new covenant with the house of Israel and the house of Judah.... *I will put my law within them, and I will write it on their hearts.* And I will be their God, and they shall be my people.[101]
>
> ....
>
> I will give you a new heart, and a new spirit I will put within you. And I will remove the heart of stone from your flesh and give you a heart of flesh.[102]
>
> ....
>
> Incline your ear, and come to me; hear, that your soul may live; and I will make with you an everlasting covenant, my steadfast, sure love for David.[103]

The day would come when God would make a new

covenant, one that would see the Law written on the hearts of his people. He would give them new hearts — hearts of "flesh" instead of "stone," hearts that yearned to please God rather than to rebel against him. God would free his people from their bondage to sin and death. He was preparing to send the one upon whom he would put his Spirit, the one "anointed ... to bring good news to the poor."[104]

Reflect, Discuss, Apply

1. Read Isaiah chapters 1 and 58. Comparing your own life against Isaiah's rebukes and appeals to repent, what patterns do you see echoed in your own life?
2. Why does it matter that justice is connected to God's character?
3. Do you agree or disagree that covenant unfaithfulness leads to ethical unfaithfulness? Why or why not?
4. What dangers do you see in the "doing enough" mindset? How can we withstand the temptation to fall into legalism while trying to compel others to care for the poor?

Five
GRACE-ENABLED SERVICE

The Gift of Love and Its Demands

It had been a long, painful journey for the Israelites. From four centuries of slavery in Egypt to a generation of wandering in the desert and, finally, to the establishment of a kingdom that was the awe of the rest of civilized world . . . now it seemed the journey was finally over. God had delivered on his promises time and again. He had made the lowly great, the simple wise, and the poor rich beyond measure.

Yet all this was still not enough for God's wayward people. Their hearts were still in bondage—not to Egypt as their forbears had been, but to sin. Repeatedly, they rebelled against God, denying his commands and ignoring his covenant. God sent prophet after prophet to plead and correct and warn them to repent, until finally his wrath was unleashed and for seventy years Israel languished in exile. Even after their return to Jerusalem, it seemed their hearts were still trapped in captivity and that God might have abandoned them altogether. Then

Malachi appeared, and with him, a new word from the Lord—a word of warning, but also of promise. God, though his anger continued to burn hot against them, had not yet given up on this stiff-necked people. He was going to send Elijah the prophet to "turn the hearts of children to their fathers, lest I come and strike the land with a decree of utter destruction."[105]

Imagine the joy the faithful must have felt upon hearing these words. What an encouragement—God was not finished with them, he had not turned his back! What a promise—what hope they must have felt!

And then? Nothing.

God was completely silent. Not another prophet; not another direct word from God. For four hundred *years,* as one oppressive regime followed another. Until one day crowds started gathering at the Jordan River, where a strange man, John, the son of Zechariah,[106] had begun teaching. His fiery message had the whole nation abuzz.

"Repent, for the kingdom of heaven is at hand," John warned.[107] "*Bear fruits in keeping with repentance. . . .* Even now the axe is laid to the root of the trees. Every tree therefore that does not bear good fruit is cut down and thrown into the fire."[108] Despite the centuries of silence, God's promises had continued to be taught and John's message echoed the warnings of the prophets of old—men like Isaiah who had warned God's people seek to justice for the oppressed and to care for the poor among them.

The weeks turned into months and men and women continued to stream in from all around the countryside to be baptized by him in the river. They confessed their sins and wanted to know how they could bear fruit in keeping with repentance. So they asked, "What then shall we do?"[109] They wanted to know what it meant to live differently in light of the change John proclaimed.

> He answered them, "Whoever has two tunics is to share with him who has none, and whoever has food is to do likewise." Tax collectors also came to be baptized and said to him, "Teacher, what shall we do?" And he said to them, "Collect no more than you are authorized to do." Soldiers also asked him, "And we, what shall we do?" And he said to them, "Do not extort money from anyone by threats or by false accusation, and be content with your wages."[110]

Do not collect more than you ought. Do not extort money. Give to those in need. These are John's instructions, each one involving economics and the practical stuff people need to live.

Sound familiar? If John had been asked to explain why he chose those three things, he might well have said something like, "Because *covenant faithfulness leads to ethical faithfulness*." We must be clear about this: John is not providing a task list and saying "Do this and you'll be right with God." He gives these instructions to people only *after* they have come to be baptized, declaring their intention and desire to turn from sin. Many of these men and women are painfully aware of their state before God. They know that they're sinners in need of a Savior. And John tells them (and us) that true repentance—turning *from* our sin and rebellion and *to* God in obedient submission — will show itself in how we care for those in need.

This again is the same message God had been giving his people since the days of Moses. God's desire is to work through his people so that the oppressed go free, the hungry have bread, and the naked are clothed. But what had happened? The land had become filled with extortionists, oppressing one another to line their own pockets, and neglecting those in need.

John's fearless preaching caused people to ask a lot of questions, of themselves and of him. Was he a sign that the Messiah was coming? Or… had he already arrived? Was *this man* the Messiah? John's answer? No. Someone else was coming, John said. Someone mighty, whose sandals he was not worthy to untie. [111] But who? The answer came quickly.

The next day as John baptized, he saw a man walking along the banks of the Jordan. John cried out, "Behold, the Lamb of God, who takes away the sin of the world!" [112] The man he saw was Jesus of Nazareth, who soon began "proclaiming the gospel of the kingdom and healing every disease and every affliction among the people." His fame grew and people brought the sick, the demon-possessed, epileptics, and paralytics to him, "and he healed them." Soon, great crowds followed him wherever he went as he "proclaimed the good news of the kingdom." And one day, seeing the crowds, he went up on a mountain, called his disciples together, and began to teach. [113]

This teaching — the Sermon on the Mount — devastated Jesus' hearers, as it continues to in our day. It completely flipped their world upside down as Jesus described what life in the kingdom of God is like.[114] The sermon's powerful ethical teaching offers us a clear understanding of what is expected of God's people—*perfection*. In your love, in your actions, in all you say, think and do, "you therefore must be perfect, as your heavenly Father is perfect."[115]

Can you imagine being part of that crowd and hearing Jesus say that God's standard is perfection? How do you measure up? But here's the good news: Jesus didn't start with the demands of citizenship. He started with grace!

First, consider the intended audience of this sermon. While some of Jesus' listeners were present merely out of curiosity, he delivered this sermon *to* and *for the benefit of* his disciples. He was not talking to neutral observers, people on the fence. He was talking to the committed.

Jesus opened his message by describing those to whom the kingdom belongs as *blessed*. He was not talking about separate categories of people—some who are meek, others who are merciful, etc. This is a single group of people sharing similar characteristics.

"Blessed are the poor in spirit ... those who mourn ... the meek ... those who hunger and thirst for righteousness ... the merciful ... the pure in heart ... the peacemakers ... those who are persecuted for righteousness' sake."[116] These are the characteristics of those who belong to the kingdom. They're men and women, boy and girls, who are painfully aware of their spiritual bankruptcy—their sinful nature that causes them to rebel against the Lord.

They know they need *grace*—and it is grace that Jesus freely offers.

We must recognize that before Jesus ever offers

ethics, he offers grace. If we don't see that then, just like the people described in Isaiah 58, we will use the Sermon on the Mount as a hammer, a means of trying to force ourselves or others to act in a way we never could act without the grace of the Holy Spirit. This legalism is the natural inclination of our hearts. We want law, not gospel. We want deeds, not creeds. We want the demands of the law—even if it's just so we can disobey them. But the good news of the gospel includes the fact that grace *always* comes before the demands of the kingdom. Jesus is not telling us what is required to earn blessing. He's telling us what to do in light of the fact that we are *already* blessed! "The gifts of love *always* precede the demands of love."[117]

That is what is so devastating about the Sermon on the Mount. It starts with *grace. Grace* kills our hypocrisy and our desire for the approval of man. *Grace* destroys our plan to try to meet God's demands out of our own will. *Grace* sweeps away our anxiety.[118] *Grace* allows us to persevere in prayer, trusting that the Father will give good gifts to those who ask. *Grace* allows us to be careful of how we judge, examining our own hearts before passing judgment on another. *Grace* allows us to put others before ourselves, doing to them what we would have them do to us.[119] To those who are weary and burdened, these words of Jesus—the grace he offers—is sweet water. To those who are proud and self-righteous, his grace is the bitterest of medicines.

This is where we have to start as we consider how to help the poor and "stir up one another to love and good works."[120] We have to start with grace. Caring for the poor starts with understanding the grace Jesus has given to those who believe in him. We must get this straight in our heads—and in our hearts.

We cannot separate what we *believe* from what we *do*. We may want to "act [our] way into a new way of thinking, not think [our] way into a new way of acting,"[121] but Jesus has not given us that luxury. We may want to proclaim "deeds, not creeds!" but Jesus has not given us that authority. We may want to separate Jesus' ethics from his identity, but Jesus has not given us that right. William Wilberforce, the famous abolitionist, warned believers of the danger of divorcing our doctrine from our deeds: "Christianity calls on us," he wrote, "not merely in general to be religious and moral, but especially to believe the doctrines, and imbibe the principles, and practice the precepts of Christ."[122]

For the Christian, Wilberforce wrote, it's not enough to be a "good," moral person. Our calling is much higher than that. We are called to believe the doctrines, drink deeply of the principles, and practice fully the precepts of Christ. What we *do* is the fruit of what we *believe* about Jesus. That's what Wilberforce is telling us above. That's what John the Baptizer taught in saying, "bear fruits in keeping with repentance." And that is what Jesus taught throughout the Sermon on the Mount.

In the same way, it's not enough that the Christian care for the needs of the poor—you don't have to be a Christian to want to help the unfortunate. As we seek to help in genuine, meaningful ways, through it all we have a greater goal: the glory of Jesus Christ.

The more I consider the question of *why* we should help the poor, the more I realize this is the answer. *We are called to care for the poor because God is glorified in our doing so.* We care for the poor because we know what it feels like to be on the receiving end of grace. *We* were the poor in spirit. *We* were lost and without hope. *We* were separated from God and enslaved to sin.

But "God so loved the world, that he gave his only Son, that whoever believes in him should not perish but have eternal life."[123] Jesus lived a life of perfect obedience to the Father, then took the punishment we deserved by dying on the cross for our sins. Jesus took our sinfulness and gave us his righteousness so that we, on the Day of Judgment, can stand confidently before God and spend eternity with him.

That is the grace he offers. That is the grace that frees us from guilt and shame over our sin. That is the grace that sustains us even in the midst of difficulty. That is the grace that enables us to consider others as greater and more important than ourselves. And that is the grace that we share when we begin to invest in the lives of the poor.

Reflect, Discuss, Apply

1. What does Jesus offer before making demands of his disciples? Why is this important?
2. Is it possible to separate Jesus' ethics from his identity? Why or why not?
3. "What we do is the fruit of what we believe about Jesus." Do you agree? Why or why not?
4. How does understanding our own spiritual poverty help us in our efforts to care for the poor?

Six
FROM DISAPPOINTMENT TO WORSHIP

Celebrating God's Plan

I have always been prone to getting songs stuck in my head. This can be especially annoying when, influenced by your season of life, the internal sonic wallpaper for the week ends up being the theme from Dora the Explorer. But there's an upside, too. Whatever it is that predisposes me to musical repetition can sometimes work just as well for Scripture repetition.

For the longest time now I've been wrestling with John 12:1-8, where Mary anoints Jesus' feet with expensive perfume and Judas objects. I can't seem to shake it. I've read the passage over and over. I've listened to powerful sermons on it and read insightful commentaries. No matter what I do, the passage won't let go. It always seems to be rattling around in the back of my head.

Six days before he is to be betrayed and brutally murdered, Jesus and his disciples stop in Bethany to visit his friend Lazarus, whose family throws a dinner party. During dinner, Mary takes "a pound of expensive ointment made from pure nard,"[124] and anoints Jesus. She pours out her most valuable earthly possession to honor Jesus in a beautiful act of worship. She sees Christ as her great treasure, whose value surpasses anything this world has to offer.

Judas has a serious problem with this; you can sense his frustration and annoyance. He says the ointment, which was worth about a year's wages, could have been sold and the money given to the poor. He's right on one level—you could do a lot of good with that kind of money. What bothers me about this passage, however, is not Judas' pragmatic argument. It's what comes next. "He said this, not because he cared about the poor, but because he was a thief, and having charge of the moneybag he used to help himself to what was put into it."[125]

Judas Iscariot may have put on a holy front, but his motives were despicably sinful. He did not love the poor; he loved money. He used the piety shtick to line his own pockets and support his own agenda. Despite having travelled with Jesus for three years—talking with him daily, eating with him, learning from him—he did not worship him. To Judas, Jesus was always "Rabbi" but never "Lord."[126] His heart was bad. He loved sin—he loved himself—more than he loved Jesus. Judas was still a child of the devil.[127]

This reminds us that not everyone who appears to have faith actually possesses it. Judas' complaint about the perfume may have been couched in a concern for the poor, but he was really only concerned for personal profit. J.C. Ryle put it well when he wrote, "A cold heart and a stingy heart will generally go together."[128]

The Poor, Always

Then Jesus drops one of his most enigmatic statements, one that still perplexes many: "Leave her alone, so that she may keep it for the day of my burial. *For the poor you always have with you, but you do not always have me.*"[129]

Jesus doesn't join in Judas' rebuke. Instead, he turns it around. "The poor you always have with you, but you do not always have me." Does this mean it's fine to have a cavalier attitude about caring for those in need? Is that the implication of "always" as it applies to the poor? Not at all, for in his gospel, Mark includes the point that we will have plenty of opportunities to "do good" to the poor[130] — not plenty of opportunities to ignore them! With his crucifixion just six days away, Jesus knew that this was literally Mary's last chance to serve him in this way and one of the last times she would be able to serve him at all before he ascended to heaven. With this one statement, Jesus is making two points — one about the poor, and one about himself.

Yet some still see "the poor you always have with you" as fatalistic, despite the clarity about this event as we find it in the larger witness of the Gospels. (*Some people will always be poor, no matter what? Then why try?*) Maybe the problem comes down to a misunderstanding about what is expected of us.

Have you ever had a goal in mind so clearly you

could almost touch it? It looks like you have green lights all the way, so you start pursuing your goal. Then everything goes sideways. Despite some disappointment, however, you still have hope. But when weeks, months, or years go by and you're still no closer to your goal, discouragement probably sets in—maybe even despair. Sooner or later, you give up.

In telling us for a fact that the poor will always be with us, perhaps Jesus is trying to set our expectations in caring for the poor. Maybe his whole point, at least as it applied to the poor, was that we might stay focused on doing good where we can.

In his commentary on John's gospel, R. C. Sproul shares the story of a minister who labored for decades in inner city Cleveland, Ohio, serving the poor, oppressed and addicted. This minister had one associate pastor after another, for none of them lasted more than about two years. Naturally, Sproul was curious, so he asked, "Why don't they last?" *Disillusionment.*

> They came out of seminary and came to the ghetto because they wanted to labor for Christ where people were hurting. But soon they became depressed and left. I asked him, "Why have you been able to stay all this time?" He said, "Because of the words of Jesus, 'The poor you have with you always.'"
>
> I replied, "Every time I've ever heard anyone quote that, it was cited as an excuse to neglect the poor, not to minister to the poor." He said: "Well, what

I understand Jesus to say is that I will never be able to eliminate poverty. Therefore, when I came here, I had no expectation that I was going to solve all these problems. I never thought I would eliminate poverty or get rid of the drug traffic or end unemployment among my parishioners. I realize that for every person that is brought out of the ghetto, more are brought in. If we get one person off of drugs, five more get hooked here. *My mission isn't to get rid of the poor or to get rid of all these problems. My mission is to minister to people who are suffering from these things while they are here and while I'm here.*"[131]

This minister saw Jesus saying "the poor you always have with you" not as a discouragement but as an *opportunity.* Because he wasn't burdened with the notion that he could end poverty in his community, he was free to fully extend the grace of God to the people he served. In telling the disciples that the poor would always be among them (and us), Jesus does us all a great service, freeing us in at least three ways to serve the poor with a biblical attitude.

Jesus' words free us from bondage to guilt over the continued existence of poverty. Let's be clear: No one with any moral or theological integrity can use Jesus' words as an excuse for dismissing the needs of the poor. This would require dismissing scores of verses *commanding* us to care for those in need. At the same time, we dare not dismiss these words as merely being for Jesus' immediate hearers in the first century. To do so would be to ignore sin's ongoing role in the persistence of poverty.

As long as sin continues on the face of the earth and in the hearts of man, there will be poverty—spiritual, material, and relational. Despite our best efforts, some people will continue to be poor. Knowing that Jesus is the only one who can truly end poverty frees us from guilt over poverty's continued existence. A day is coming when Jesus *will* end poverty forever, but it won't be through us.[132]

Jesus' words free us to love the poor unconditionally. Humanistic goals like ending extreme global poverty within our lifetime add a condition to our caring for the poor. Ministry that should be focused on people instead becomes focused on targets. Targets aren't bad in themselves, but they can be devastating to those we're trying to help, and to Christian service in general.

As Christians, our agenda should be to see rebellious sinners reconciled to the Father.[133] That *includes* doing what we can to minister to the poor amid their suffering, but it obviously goes well beyond it as well. Our ultimate desire should be to see God glorified as he becomes their Savior.

The alternative is that we become the savior, with the attitude Corbett and Fikkert call "paternalism."[134] To assume that our knowledge, resources, and processes are all that's needed to fix the problems of the poor is a recipe for self-glorification. If you do not point the poor to the one who can save them from spiritual poverty, the only thing you will point to is yourself—your own wealth, wisdom, kindness, and glory.

Jesus' words free us to worship him joyfully through our care for the poor. Ultimately, caring for the poor is a worship issue. As we saw in chapter four, caring for the poor is central to the true worship of God. While Jesus tells us that we cannot trust in the things we do as proof of our salvation, he *does* say that a sign—even *the* sign—of our love for him is our love for each other, including those in need within the Church.[135] A cold heart may lead to a closed hand, but a warm heart—one made alive through the power of the Holy Spirit—always leads to an open hand to those in need.

When we see the horrifying needs that exist in the world, whether caused by natural disaster or human dysfunction, we need not despair nor become discouraged. Our hope for a better world in this lifetime is in Christ. There is a *role* for social action, but our hope is not *in* social action. The poor always with us means we have virtually endless opportunities to practically worship Christ, expressing our love for God through caring for the poor of this world.

Serving the Poor and the End of the Age

Once Jesus ascended, no one would be able to serve him directly in a three-dimensional, physical way like Mary did with her anointing ointment. But the poor *are* still with us, and service to the poor is a kind of service to Jesus. It is no coincidence that Jesus spoke of service to him and service to the poor in the same breath. Real-time, physical service to the poor is a form of real-time, physical service to Jesus. Does this seem like a stretch? Consider what Jesus himself says will happen when he returns:

When the Son of Man comes in his glory, and all
the angels with him, then he will sit on his glorious
throne. Before him will be gathered all the nations,
and he will separate people one from another as a
shepherd separates the sheep from the goats. And
he will place the sheep on his right, but the goats on
the left. Then the King will say to those on his right,
"Come, you who are blessed by my Father, inherit the
kingdom prepared for you from the foundation of
the world. For I was hungry and you gave me food,
I was thirsty and you gave me drink, I was a stranger
and you welcomed me, I was naked and you clothed
me, I was sick and you visited me, I was in prison
and you came to me." Then the righteous will answer
him, saying, "Lord, when did we see you hungry and
feed you, or thirsty and give you drink? And when
did we see you a stranger and welcome you, or naked
and clothe you? And when did we see you sick or
in prison and visit you?" And the King will answer
them, "Truly, I say to you, *as you did it to one of the
least of these my brothers, you did it to me.*"

Then he will say to those on his left, "Depart from me,
you cursed, into the eternal fire prepared for the devil
and his angels. For I was hungry and you gave me no
food, I was thirsty and you gave me no drink, I was a
stranger and you did not welcome me, naked and you
did not clothe me, sick and in prison and you did not
visit me." Then they also will answer, saying, "Lord,
when did we see you hungry or thirsty or a stranger

or naked or sick or in prison, and did not minister to
you?" Then he will answer them, saying, "Truly, I say
to you, *as you did not do it to one of the least of these,
you did not do it to me.*" And these will go away into
eternal punishment, but the righteous into eternal
life.[136]

The righteous are confused. They say, "Jesus, when
did we see you? When did we serve you?" They had
simply been going about their business as believers in
Christ, but because they were living life with a changed
heart, they found themselves reaching out to and helping
those less fortunate than themselves. Their covenant
faithfulness worked itself out so naturally in ethical faithfulness that *they didn't even realize it was happening.*

We must come to terms with this. *When the poor,
whom Christ considers his brothers, suffer in any way,
Christ suffers, and to serve them is, in some mysterious way,
to serve Christ.* This includes the poor suffer because, by
human standards, they seem to deserve it, such as people
in prison. The connection to the story of Mary and the
ointment is profound: *to serve the poor is to serve Christ.*
Is this not exactly what Jesus says above as well?

What about Jesus' use of the phrase "my brothers"?
Can we conclude that those who do not currently possess
faith in Christ are excluded from the scope of our care? By
no means—such an idea would violate our Lord's own
teaching, which we examined in the last chapter. While
"my brothers" does indicate those among who are among
the *visible* Church, it also applies to the *invisible*. At this

moment, only God knows which particular individuals among the lost will ultimately be among the multitude spending eternity with him.[137] All these he has loved and chosen from the foundation of the world.[138] And because you and I do not know who belongs to Christ, we dare not hold back his love from any who may be among "the least of these."

Are you interested in serving Jesus? Had you been there in Jerusalem, would you have envied Mary for the extravagance and beauty of her worship? Then our Lord has a solution—you have unlimited opportunities to serve the poor in his place! To serve them *is* to serve him!

Once again, this is not a matter of salvation by works. Rather, it underscores a cornerstone idea of this book: covenant faithfulness simply results in ethical faithfulness, often in ways that are so natural we don't even notice.

I want you to see the unique opportunities God has placed before you—opportunities to serve others for his glory and your joy. Maybe a place to start is by taking one night this week to help at your local street mission, intentionally getting to know one person being assisted there. Maybe it's talking to the local men's or women's shelters about how you or your church can be a resource. Maybe it's supporting a child who lives in poverty through a reputable Christian organization. If you stop and look, the opportunities are virtually limitless.

"The poor you always have with you"—will you see this as an opportunity to worship the one who sacrificed all for you?

Reflect, Discuss, Apply

1. We should see Jesus saying, "The poor you always have with you," not as a discouragement but as an opportunity. Do you agree or disagree? Why?
2. Why does Jesus put such a strong emphasis on caring for the needs of "the least of these brothers of mine"? What does our care for others tell us about our hearts?
3. Brainstorm a series of practical ways you and your church can practically assist the poor, whether locally or globally. Which could you realistically pursue?

Seven
A THANKFUL HEART

The Holy Spirit, Generosity and Getting Past "Enough"

Not too long ago, I was sitting in a conference for church leaders. From our simulcast location, the host came on the screen, asking for an offering to help pay for providing the conference's teaching resources to poor leaders around the globe. Just before the offering was taken, he looked to the audience, sternly pointed a finger and declared, "If you aren't giving your full ten percent to your local church, don't give to this. You are in sin and you are robbing God. Get right with God and then give to this."

I've heard a lot of similar comments over the years, but this time it just made me angry, and I spent months wondering why. After a great deal of prayer and searching the Scriptures, I realized I wasn't angry because I was being convicted of sin in this area. I was angry because this attitude turns financial giving—something that should be a wonderful, worshipful act—into something ugly. This is a common example of the "doing enough" mindset we discussed in chapter four—only in this instance, it's being used to club the hearers into submitting to a questionable view of giving to your church.[139] "If you're not giving your full ten percent, you are in sin and robbing God." Does that actually inspire generosity? From what I can see, it leads only to pride or despair.

If I'm giving "my full ten percent" and because of it I am somehow "right with God," I've abandoned grace. All it does is give me a supposed reason to boast.[140] "Yes, Jesus died on the cross to pay the penalty for my sins, but it's my giving that makes me right with God in the end." Even worse, if I'm not giving ten percent, then I'm a sponge who doesn't have enough faith in God to provide for my needs.

Driven by bad theology, I've been both of these people. I've been proud of going above the magic number 10, and I've felt beaten up about "not having enough faith" to give away our grocery money when we were learning how to budget again with one income. Both these versions of the "enough" perspective are ugly. Both are sinful. Neither one encourages us to love Jesus more. Yet the variations on the "enough" approach frequently underlie organizational efforts to motivate us to care for the poor, both locally and globally. Why?

Sometimes I wonder if it comes down to unbelief— that churches, parachurch groups, and organizations (I am obviously limiting my comments to explicitly Christian efforts here) don't trust that God's grace and the Holy Spirit are powerful enough to make people generous. I want to be clear on this: people *should* be challenged to give generously and to reexamine whether or not they're doing so. But let's avoid a mindset of always trying to figure out how much is "enough." The question should never be, "am I doing enough?" It should be, "If God requires more of me, will I respond in faith?" The best and most biblical scenario, I believe, is when we allow God's grace and the power of the Holy Spirit to motivate generosity.

Generosity by the Spirit

Soon after Jesus ascends into heaven, we see something amazing in the book of Acts: the Holy Spirit comes in power. A small, fearful band of believers hiding behind a locked door is suddenly filled with the Holy Spirit and immediately emerges to proclaim the gospel boldly to all Jerusalem. In the streets, Peter begins to preach:

> Men of Israel, hear these words: Jesus of Nazareth, a man attested to you by God with mighty works and wonders and signs that God did through him in your midst, as you yourselves know — this Jesus, delivered up according to the definite plan and foreknowledge of God, you crucified and killed by the hands of lawless men. God raised him up, loosing the pangs of death, because it was not possible for him to be held by it.[141]

Peter spoke with power and conviction. His words "cut to the heart" of his hearers, who asked, "Brothers, what shall we do?" Peter responded, "Repent and be baptized every one of you in the name of Jesus Christ for the forgiveness of your sins, and you will receive the gift of the Holy Spirit." And three *thousand* people joined them that day.[142]

Can you imagine what that must have been like? Not just to see three thousand people come to faith in Jesus, but to see the change in a man like Peter? He went from being terrified of a little girl[143] to telling a crowd of thousands that they were going to face the wrath of God unless they repented and believed in Jesus!

The apostles, following their baptism in the Spirit, went about proclaiming Christ in Jerusalem, and every day more were added to the church. The Holy Spirit was bringing men, women, and children to faith in Jesus, regardless of social class. Those who saw what was happening were awed by the miracles taking place. But there was something else—genuine community began to form. "They devoted themselves to the apostles' teaching and the fellowship, to the breaking of bread and the prayers," Luke wrote.[144]

> And all who believed were together and had all things in common. And they were selling their possessions and belongings and distributing the proceeds to all, as any had need. And day by day, attending the temple together and breaking bread in their homes, they received their food with glad and generous hearts, praising God and having favor with all the people. And the Lord added to their number day by day those who were being saved.[145]

So strong was the bond between these believers that they had a great desire to meet one another's needs.

Nothing was off-limits. Homes and lives were open. People were giving away what they had, exchanging their earthly treasures for treasure in heaven. It's amazing to consider, possibly because the whole concept is so foreign to those of us living in the western world.

What's going on in this picture of the early church? Was it some form of proto-communist experiment? There is no record of anyone suggesting that they do this, much less commanding it. Despite what some proponents of poverty theology might suggest, personal property was not seen as wicked or sinful in the early church. Indeed, even during this time, many believers continued to own homes where they would meet (see v 46), and Acts 5:4 indicates that the believers were under no obligation to relieve themselves of all their earthly possessions.

So why this outpouring of generosity? It was motivated by the grace of God. It was a spontaneous response to God's lavish generosity toward them in not holding back the most precious treasure of all—free and unmerited salvation through the Son. No command or guilt trip can inspire the openhanded lifestyle.

This is the pattern throughout the Bible: God's grace motivates generosity in his people. In Genesis 14:19-20, Abram gives Melchizedek a tenth of his spoils, but there is no command to do so. It's motivated by Abram's love for God and his conviction that Melchizedek is God's special servant.

In Exodus, as plans are made for the construction of the tabernacle, God says, "From every man *whose heart moves him* you shall receive the contribution for me."[146]

Moses then tells the Israelites, "Take from among you a contribution to the Lord. *Whoever is of a generous heart*, let him bring the Lord's contribution." When the people returned, they had to be restrained from giving, as what they offered was far beyond what was needed![147]

In Second Corinthians, which contains perhaps the most exhaustive instruction on New Covenant giving, we read about a similarly generous offering. There, Paul commends the Macedonians to the Corinthians, saying that though they were in serious affliction and extreme poverty, they gave in an overflow of *generosity according to their means*.[148] Paul was taking up a collection (as he mentions in nearly all his epistles) to help the impoverished Jerusalem church, and the Macedonians responded with overflowing generosity. Paul seeks to encourage the Corinthians to do likewise, explaining:

> The point is this: whoever sows sparingly will also reap sparingly, and whoever sows bountifully will also reap bountifully. Each one must give as he has decided in his heart, not reluctantly or under compulsion, for God loves a cheerful giver. And God is able to make all grace abound to you, so that having all sufficiency in all things at all times, you may abound in every good work. As it is written, "He has distributed freely, he has given to the poor; his righteousness endures forever."
>
> He who supplies seed to the sower and bread for food will supply and multiply your seed for sowing

and increase the harvest of your righteousness. You will be enriched in every way for all your generosity, which through us will produce thanksgiving to God. For the ministry of this service is not only supplying the needs of the saints but is also overflowing in many thanksgivings to God. [149]

What is Paul saying here? While space prevents an in-depth examination of the text, we can see that he's laying out a number of straightforward principles—at least four positive and one negative—that should guide how we give. The positive principles are these:

- Give generously (v 6).
- Give according to what you've decided in your heart (v 7a).
- Give cheerfully (v 7c).
- Give with a thankful heart (vv 11-12)

The negative principle is simple: *do not give under compulsion* (v 7b). Giving out of a sense of guilt or external pressure isn't generosity: it's extortion, and God will have none of it. All of our giving is to be from a generous heart, cheerfully offered. Guilt and obligation don't produce this kind of heart, but the Holy Spirit does. Grace produces generosity as men and women are reminded of the gospel—that Jesus, though he was rich became poor on our behalf, lived a sinless life, died on the cross, offering up his life for ours, and rose again to give us the gift of new life.

Statistics won't do it. Telling people they need a conversion of their wallets won't do it. Telling them to "fake it until they make it" won't do it. But reminding them of God's generosity towards them—that will melt the heart of a true believer, every time.

Guidelines for Giving

When we talk about helping the poor, it is for good reason that we tend to think in terms of financial sacrifice: without such sacrifice, very little of substance can be accomplished. But generosity is about much more than money. As a Christian, your entire life is supposed to be an act of generosity—a life invested in, spent for, and used up to the glory of God and the good of others. So by way of application, here are a few principles that can help guide financial, material, and relational giving to care for the needs of the poor.

Should I Give At All?

This comes down to a question of desire. Do you *want* to give? This is completely apart from the question of whether you can see it "working" or not. Would you *like* to give, or are you mainly interested in keeping it all—your resources, your time, and your talents—for yourself? We have seen in Scripture that in the heart of every true believer is a deep desire to be generous to others with their time, talents, and treasures. If your inclination is to find some passage you can isolate from the rest of Scripture and spin a little as a way of justifying a lack of generosity, I would encourage you to examine your heart.

Matthew 6:21 rightly tells us that "where your treasure is, there your heart will be also."

James underscored the fact that believers have a natural generosity when he wrote,

> What good is it, my brothers, if someone says he has faith but does not have works? Can that faith save him? If a brother or sister is poorly clothed and lacking in daily food, and one of you says to them, "Go in peace, be warmed and filled," without giving them the things needed for the body, what good is that? So also faith by itself, if it does not have works, is dead.[150]

A true believer cannot simply pretend the legitimate material needs of others don't exist or don't matter. They may not be able to meet all such needs, nor are they called to do so, but they will always have an inclination to seek to meet what needs they can, whether through their time, talents, treasures, or relationships. (See the Appendix.)

Within this question also lies an issue of wisdom. Sometimes it is unwise to assist an individual financially. Sometimes, it can be the least merciful thing you could do. For example, you don't give your alcoholic uncle money if you know he will use to buy booze instead of bread. To do so would be enabling his poverty, not alleviating it. But you can be generous relationally, expressing your concern for his wellbeing and sharing the gospel's promise of freedom from bondage to sin and new life in Jesus. As in all things, prayer and counsel from other believers should help guide you in addressing complicated situations.

To Whom Should I Give?

One's family. Biblically, the first priority for all believers is to provide for the needs of his or her family. "But if anyone does not provide for his relatives, and especially for members of his household, he has denied the faith and is worse than an unbeliever."[151] This does not mean that we provide whatever our families want—refusing your kids an Xbox, for example, is not a violation of this command—but that we do everything we can to ensure they lack nothing in terms of necessities, with the definition of "necessities" varying widely depending on factors such as number and age of children, family resources, how the children are educated, etc.

The family of God. The second priority for all believers is to provide for the needs of the family of God—the Church. "Let us do good to everyone, and especially to those who are of the household of faith," Paul commands.[152] If a family or individual in our church has a need that's been made known, we as a church body have a responsibility to help them. Helping to care for the needs of those whom God calls into full-time ministry also falls into this category.

The world. The third priority for the believer is caring for the needs of the world at large. This sphere tends to be the focus of charitable organizations and parachurch ministries. There are many fantastic organizations serving the poor, so it's easy to be overwhelmed with choices. In choosing which, if any, to support, there at least three factors to consider:

- First and foremost, give to organizations that demonstrate Christ's love, not only in practical ways but also by explicitly sharing the gospel with those they serve. "Deed ministry" and "Word ministry" cannot be divorced. It is not enough to give a child clean drinking water; that child also needs "living water."[153]
- Equally important is an organization's ability to prove its trustworthiness. How do they handle money? Can they prove that what they say they do actually happens? This is ultimately a wisdom issue.
- Finally, consider whether or not their goals and methods resonate with your values. If what you really care about is giving people clean water (along with the gospel), then do it. If you care about seeing a little boy or girl go to school, do it. If your heart is for training pastors in the developing world, do it. Get involved in whatever cause you find motivating.

How Much Should I Give?

Use prayerful wisdom. Whether considering time or treasures, this is between you and the Lord. Paul tells each man to "give as he has decided in his heart." Typically, charities recommend financial gifts that are based on the real costs of their programs. In those instances it is wise to honor the numbers they provide. But if your means allow you only to offer a "small" gift, do so. A gift given cheerfully and with thanksgiving might be small in the eyes of man, but it's great in the eyes of God.[154]

Please hear my heart on this issue—my desire is not

to throw rocks at those who are trying to encourage Christians about their giving. I have to believe their motives are genuinely good. It's only that some common approaches can be biblically misguided and therefore unhelpful. But the truth is clear, and more than sufficient: God has been infinitely generous to us in not sparing the greatest treasure of all, Jesus Christ. And because he has been so generous to us, we cannot hesitate in being generous to others, ministering to those in need with deeds of mercy and words of grace, introducing them to the Savior whom we know, and for whom we wait.

Reflect, Discuss, Apply

1. How has God's grace motivated generosity in you? Don't limit your answer to financial matters.
2. "It is not enough to give a child clean drinking water; that child also needs 'living water.'" Do you agree? Why or why not?
3. What other factors (beyond those discussed in this chapter) do you think should be considered as you try to determine which charitable organization(s) to support?

Eight

WIPING EVERY TEAR

The End of Poverty and an Eternity with Jesus

"He's too heavenly minded to be of any earthly good." As often as I hear that cliché, I want to cringe. If "heavenly minded" is sometimes used as a synonym for "dreamy and unfocused," that's one thing—but to be truly heavenly minded is to be clear-eyed, motivated, inspired, and practical in a way that no other perspective can match.

The Bible actively *encourages* and indeed commands us to be heavenly minded:

- If you have been raised with Christ, "seek the things that are above, where Christ is. . . . Set your minds on things that are above, not on things that are on earth."[155]
- We are "born again . . . to an inheritance that is imperishable, undefiled, and unfading, kept in heaven."[156]
- "Bear the image of the man of heaven."[157]
- Look to "wisdom from above" and embrace the

freedom from sin that comes from "the Jerusalem above."[158]

- "Let us . . . draw near to the throne of grace," which resides in heaven, and wait for the "Son from heaven."[159]

Over and over again, New Testament authors tell us to keep our focus on heaven.

The book of Philippians contains one of the greatest of these exhortations. After warning against following the example of the self-righteous, who have their "minds set on earthly things,"[160] Paul writes, "But our citizenship is in heaven, and from it we await a Savior, the Lord Jesus Christ, who will transform our lowly body to be like his glorious body, by the power that enables him even to subject all things to himself."[161]

Here Paul tells us not simply that we ought to look to heaven, but that heaven is where we have our citizenship. How can we *not* look there? We are citizens of the kingdom of God, not of this world. We should not trust our accomplishments and abilities like those who "glory in their shame"—we instead "await a Savior, the Lord Jesus Christ." We should not spend time trying to figure out how to make ourselves perfect but should trust in his power to "transform our lowly body to be like his glorious body." That makes all the difference in how we approach work, relationships, ministry, and even how we respond to the needs of the poor.

From the earliest days of the Church, Christians were motivated by God's generosity towards them to minister to those in need with acts of mercy and the word of grace. Christopher Wordsworth explains:

> The pleadings of Christian Apologists for the Faith against Jewish and Gentile opponents were allied with the powerful and persuasive arguments of the moral, social, and spiritual influence of Christianity, as contrasted with Heathenism, in daily life and manners ... in the elevation of Womanhood ... and in the gradual abolition of Slavery, and in the ransoming of Captives, and in acts of mercy and love to the sick and dying in Hospitals, and in times of Plagues, Pestilences, and Famines.... These things preached the Divine Truth of Christianity with silent eloquence, and won for it a thousand hearts.[162]

Even the first Council of Nicaea decreed that wherever a cathedral or church was built, a hospital would be as well. Those hospitals would be open to the poor, the working class, and the elderly and infirm—both within the church and without. So strong was their influence that it shamed Roman Emperor Julian the Apostate, who wrote to Arsacius, the pagan high priest of Galatia:

> Why do we not look to that which has been the principal cause of the augmentation of impiety, care in burying the dead, and that sanctity of life, of which [Christians] make such a show? ... For it is a shame, when ... the impious Galileans [Christians] relieve not only their own people, but ours also, that our

poor should be neglected by us, and be left helpless and destitute.[163]

Adoption, education, law—there is no area of life where the fruit of Christians' heavenly mindedness, the influence of Jesus working through his people, cannot be seen. The witness of the saints of old—men and women who endured horrific persecution, suffering, and death— is a powerful reminder of the truth that having one's mind "above" allows us to be of the utmost earthly good.

That is the fruit of heavenly mindedness. But it is not the hope.

The hope is found in the final book of the Bible, Revelation. Through his vision's powerful imagery and symbolism, the apostle John gives us a glimpse of what is to come when the Lord returns: great tribulation and vindication for God's people, judgment for God's enemies, and the restoration and renewal of creation. "Behold, I am making all things new," says Jesus from his throne. "Write this down, for these words are trustworthy and true."[164]

I saw a new heaven and a new earth, for the first heaven and the first earth had passed away, and the sea was no more. And I saw the holy city, new Jerusalem, coming down out of heaven from God, prepared as a bride adorned for her husband. And I heard a loud voice from the throne saying, "Behold, the dwelling place of God is with man. He will dwell with them, and they will be his people, and God himself will be with them as their God. He will wipe away every tear from their eyes, and death shall be no more, neither shall there be mourning, nor crying, nor pain anymore, for the former things have passed away."[165]

The new Jerusalem will come out of heaven. There, God will dwell with man in a renewed creation where we will live forever—working, eating, playing, and building relationships to the glory of God. Our lost identities, our broken relationship with God, our devastated relationships with one another, our ruined relationship with the world—all will be finally and fully restored on that day. There will be no more death, no mourning or crying and no pain. All these will have passed away and Jesus himself "will wipe away every tear from [our] eyes.

"We can hardly imagine that the effects of sin can ever be removed," writes William Hendriksen. "Yet they are going to be taken away so that all things shall actually be made 'new.' To strengthen us in our faith that He who promised will really do it, we read, 'Behold!'"[166] That is the hope to which we look in our heavenly mindedness. And it's the hope that we consider as we conclude our study of poverty and the Christian response. Without the hope of the coming of the new creation, we have nothing to offer those who suffer in poverty. It is this hope we must share, whether we're working for relief, development, or social reform.[167]

We must bring immediate relief to those suffering from severe drought and famine, but we must also bring them the promise that there is one who will someday relieve all their suffering. We must give the young man who has been trapped in a familial cycle of crime and poverty the skills he needs to leave the system, but we must also offer him the promise of a new identity that comes from the one who died for his sins. We must confront a social system that abuses and breaks the backs of its people, but we must also share the promise of a world where perfect peace and justice will reign forever. And if at times we must do that despite some governmental system that forbids gospel content, so be it.

"He will dwell with them, and they will be his people, and God himself will be with them as their God." This is the hope of all Christians from the first days of the Church. This is the hope that allowed the saints of old to give their lives for the cause of Christ. It is the best of all possible hopes we can offer the poor. The hope for an eternal end to poverty—one not found in human effort, but in the return of Jesus, when he will make all things new and wipe away every tear from every eye.

This is no empty hope. It is a promise from the very mouth of our Lord and Savior. He will do it, as surely as he has promised that he is coming soon. Will we join in sharing that hope? Will we put aside our man-centered goals and desires that ultimately lead to disillusionment? Will we throw away empty promises and earthly ideas of success, instead trusting that Christ will do what he has promised? Some of his people suffer now, but they "shall hunger no more, neither thirst anymore. . . . For the Lamb . . . will be their shepherd, and he will guide them to springs of living water."[168]

Will we look to heaven and see that reality coming? Will we share that promise? Will we, with thankful hearts for the mercy that God has shown us, extend mercy in word and deed to those who so desperately need it, whether they're down the street or across the globe? Will we set our minds not on "earthly things" but on "the things that are above" as we join our voices with those of all the saints, saying, "Come, Lord Jesus"?[169]

That is my hope and prayer for us all. May God give us the grace to see it through.

Reflect, Discuss, Apply

1. What is the fruit of heavenly mindedness? Are our minds set more on earthly things or the things that are above?
2. As you consider this chapter and everything you've learned through this study, how has your view of helping the poor been changed?

Appendix
WHAT TO DO NOW

When we look at the needs of the poor and the vast number of organizations seeking to meet those needs, it's easy to become overwhelmed. In order to help you as you evaluate how you can best serve the poor, I want to leave you with the following practical reminders.

Not all Christians are called to serve the poor in the same way or to the same extent. While every believer *is* called to show concern for the poor, the practical expressions of that concern will differ from one person to another. Some of us are called to immerse ourselves fully in ministries of mercy; others, less so. Our investment in mercy ministry neither establishes nor reflects our holiness, dedication to the Lord, or sensitivity to God's Spirit. Be faithful in serving where God has called you.

You are not called to meet every need. You can only meet the needs God has given you an ability to address. Remember, it's not a question of doing "enough." We are called to live open-handed lives, willing to give of our time and treasure as the Lord directs.

Don't allow selfishness to masquerade as humility. If God makes you aware of a need that seems to be a little outside your skill set or your comfort zone, it may still be that he wants you to stretch, in his grace, and try to meet that need. When we are weak, God is strong, and those whom we serve can often sense if we are serving in our own strength, or in the grace that God provides.

Look for simple, practical ways to serve. Regardless of where you live, there are more needs around you than you realize. Some needs are best met through your participation in an existing organization, but many others can be met by your own simple acts of mercy. Ask God to give you eyes to see and a heart to serve.

Work with experts you can trust. There are many individuals and organizations working to alleviate the suffering of the poor, whether locally or globally. Their expertise is rare and invaluable. Do your homework—read whatever material is available on their work and carefully review their finances to ensure they are good stewards of the money entrusted to them. CharityNavigator.org is an extremely helpful resource for identifying trustworthy charitable organizations.

Spiritual problems require spiritual solutions. If the root of poverty is sin, man-made solutions won't bring end it. Christ will be the one to end poverty, first spiritually and finally materially in the new creation. Therefore, look to organizations that are committed to the Church and are faithfully proclaiming the gospel in word, even as they minister to the physical and relational needs of the poor.

Trust God for the results. Remember, your job is not to end poverty, but to minister to those who are suffering. Do what you can and prayerfully trust God for the results.

Acknowledgments

Much appreciation goes out Amber Van Schooneveld and Andrew Hall for their input throughout the process of writing this book. Thanks also to Kevin, Tim, and Bob at Cruciform for allowing me to share this material with you. To my colleagues Adam, John, Eric, and Sara, I'm grateful for your support and occasional kibitzing. Thanks to our church family at Harvest Bible Chapel London for all their prayers—and especially to those in the Tuesday morning prayer group who have had to listen to me yammer on about this for months on end.

To my wife, Emily, thank you for allowing me the time to write this book. You've been incredibly patient and I can't thank you enough (aside from honoring your request that I take some time off before starting another big project). And to my daughters, Abigail and Hannah— Daddy's all done now, girls.

Finally, thank you for reading this book. I hope it's been helpful for you and I'm praying that God would use it in your life both for his glory and your joy.

Endnotes

1. TheRealIssue.ca, accessed February 19, 2011, http://www.therealissue.ca
2. TheRealIssue.ca, "Get Involved," accessed February 19, 2011, http://www.therealissue.ca/get-involved.
3. One.org, "ONE History," accessed February 19, 2011, http://one.org/c/international/about/944.
4. Psalm 51:5
5. See, for example, Galatians 6:10, 1 John 3:17-18, and James 2:17.

6. Genesis 1:3, 6-7, 9, 11, 14-15, 20-21, 24
7. Genesis 1:10, 12, 18, 21, 25
8. Genesis 1:26-27
9. Genesis 1:28
10. Genesis 1:31
11. Genesis 2:20-25
12. cf. Revelation 12:9; 20:2
13. Genesis 3:1b
14. Genesis 3:2-3
15. Genesis 3:4-5
16. Genesis 3:6-7
17. cf. Ephesians 2:1-3
18. Rom. 5:12
19. Genesis 3:11-13
20. Genesis 3:16
21. Genesis3:17-19
22. Exodus 32:23-24
23. 1 Samuel 2:12-36
24. 2 Samuel 13:1-33, 15-18
25. Jeffrey D. Sachs, *The End of Poverty: Economic Possibilities for Our Time* (Penguin, 2006), 288-308. The US had pledged to contribute 0.7% GDP, but was not giving at that level when Sachs' wrote. To do so today would require borrowed capital.
26. Paul Collier, *The Bottom Billion* (Oxford U. Press, 2007), 176.
27. Sean Astin as Mikey in *The Goonies* (1985). Watch this scene online at http://www.youtube.com/watch?v=6NEKzLiXfuc.
28. Genesis 4:1
29. Genesis 3:14-15
30. Genesis 4:3-25
31. "Enoch walked with God, and he was not, for God took him" (Genesis 5:24). Enoch is one of two people in Scripture who do not taste death (the other is the prophet Elijah—see 2 Kings 2:11).
32. Genesis 5:5, 8, 11, 14, 17, 20, 27, 31
33. Genesis 6:5-7
34. The Hebrew word translated "favor" here (Genesis 6:8) is the word for "grace." This is significant as this marks the first time the word "grace" appears in the entire Bible. It also reminds us that God's saving actions are the same yesterday, today, and

forever—all are saved by grace through faith. For a helpful exposition of grace in Noah's life, see *"But God…"* by Casey Lute (Cruciform Press, 2011), 9-17.

35. Genesis 6:13-22

36. Genesis 8:1-22

37. Genesis 8:21-22

38. Micah 3:2, Ephesians 5:11

39. UNDP.org, "Where Do We Stand," accessed June 17, 2011, http://www.beta.undp.org/undp/en/home/mdgoverview/mdg_goals/mdg1/Where_do_we_stand.html.

40. 1 John 2:16

41. UNDP.org, "Where Do We Stand."

42. Genesis 9:1, 11:1

43. Genesis 11:4b

44. CQTranscripts, "Obama 'Still Fired Up' After Tough Loss in N.H. Primary," WashingtonPost.com, January 8, 2008, http://www.washingtonpost.com/wp-dyn/content/article/2008/01/08/AR2008010804032.html.

45. Steve Corbett and Brian Fikkert, *When Helping Hurts* (Moody, 2009), 65.

46. Romans 7:21

47. Genesis 11:5-7

48. R. Kent Hughes, *Genesis: Beginning and Blessings* (Crossway, 2004), Kindle edition.

49. The Millennium Development Goals are to 1. Eradicate extreme poverty and hunger. 2. Achieve universal primary education 3. Promote gender equality and empower women 4. Reduce child mortality 5. Improve maternal health 6. Combat HIV/AIDS, malaria and other diseases 7. Ensure environmental sustainability 8. Develop a global partnership for development. For more details, see UNDP.org, "Millennium Development Goals," accessed June 16, 2011, http://www.beta.undp.org/undp/en/home/mdgoverview.html.

50. Sachs, *The End of Poverty*, 25.

51. Collier, *The Bottom Billion*, 192.

52. Hughes, *Genesis: Beginning and Blessings*

53. Genesis 11:9

54. Sachs, *The End of Poverty*, 328.

55. Adam: Genesis 1:27, 2:16-17 (cf. Hosea 6:7). Noah: Genesis 9:8-9. Abraham: Genesis 12:7, 17:1-14, 22:15-19 (cf. Galatians 3:6). Moses and Israel: Exodus3:4-10, 6:7-8, 19:5. God also makes covenants with David (2 Samuel 7:8, cf. Psalm 89:3) and promises the New Covenant (Jeremiah 31:31-34, cf. Matthew 26:26-29).

56. The moral law is typified in theTen Commandments (Exodus 20:1-21); the social law is found in Exodus 21:1-23:13; the ceremonial law in Exodus 25:1-31:18 and Leviticus 1:1- 27:34.

57. Deuteronomy 7:8b

58. Deuteronomy 7:11

59. See Leviticus 20:22-26; Psalm 86:8-10; 96:3-6, 10; 117; Isaiah 42:6.

60. Deuteronomy 15:1-3

61. Deuteronomy 15:4-6

62. Deuteronomy 15:7-8, 11

63. Deuteronomy 9:6b

64. Deuteronomy 15:9-10

65. Deuteronomy 15:3

66. Exodus 22:21, 23:9; Leviticus 19:10, 23:22

67. Deuteronomy 10:17-19

68. See Proverbs 6:10-11, 21:25, 24:30-34; 1Timothy 5:8.

69. Deuteronomy 7:7-8; 9:6, 13-29; Exodus 32:9-10, 15

70. Deuteronomy 4:9, 23; 6:12; 8:11; 11:16; 12:13, 19, 30; 15:9

71. cf. Leviticus 26:41; Jeremiah 9:26; Ezekiel 44:7, 9; Acts 7:51; Romans 1:18-25

72. Deuteronomy 18:15-22, 34:10

73. Judges 21:25

74. 1 Kings

75. 1 Kings 11:6; 14:22; 15:26, 34; 16:25; 22:52; 2 Kings 3:2; 8:18, 27; 13:2, 11; 14:24; 15:9, 18, 24, 28; 17:2; 21:2, 16, 20; 23:32, 37; 24:9, 19

76. Ezekiel 14:6, 18:30

77. 2Timothy 3:4; cf. Amos 4:1

78. Isaiah 58:2-3a

79. Isaiah 58:3b-5

80. Isaiah 1:11, 13-15

81. cf. Psalm 66:18

82. Isaiah 58:6-7

83. Amos 4:1-5

84. Jeremiah 2:34-35a
85. Ezekiel 16:49-52
86. Genesis 19:5
87. Isaiah 1:17, 58:9b-10
88. Amos 5:23-24
89. Wayne Grudem, *Systematic Theology: An Introduction to Biblical Doctrine* (Zondervan, 1994), 20.
90. Deuteronomy 32:4
91. 1 Samuel 15:22
92. John 14:15
93. Matthew 22:37-40
94. Luke 10:29-37
95. Raymond C. Ortlund, Jr., Isaiah: God Saves Sinners (Wheaton: Crossway, 2005), Kindle edition.
96. James makes this connection in James 2:14-26 when he writes that "faith apart from works is dead" (v 26; cf. v 17).
97. Matthew 3:8, Luke 3:8
98. WorldHunger.org, "Hunger in America: 2011 United States Hunger and Poverty Facts," accessed July 17, 2011, http://www.worldhunger.org/articles/Learn/us_hunger_facts.htm. In the United States, "extreme poverty" is defined as a family of four living on less than $10,000 annually.
99. Isaiah 64:6
100. Ortlund, *Isaiah: God Saves Sinners*
101. Jeremiah 31:31, 33
102. Ezekiel 36:26 (cf. 11:19)
103. Isaiah 55:3
104. Isaiah 61:1
105. Malachi 4:5-6
106. Luke 3:2
107. Matt. 3:2
108. Luke 3:8-9 (emphasis added)
109. Matt. 3:5-6
110. Luke 3:10-14
111. Luke 3:16-17
112. John 1:29
113. Matt 4:17; 23-25; 5:1
114. For a thorough examination, I wholeheartedly recommend D.

Martyn Lloyd-Jones' *Studies in the Sermon on the Mount* and D. A. Carson's *Jesus' Sermon on the Mount*.

115. See Matthew 5:17-48.

116. Matthew 5:2-10

117. Ted Hamilton, "One-ist Social Justice," delivered January 6, 2011, at the 2011 Truth Xchange ThinkTank in Escondido, California, http://truthxchange.com/wp-content/uploads/2011/03/1-6-2011_Hamilton_One-ist%20Social%20Justice.mp3.

118. Matthew 6:1-34

119. Matthew 7:1-12

120. Hebrews 10:24

121. Jim Wallis, as quoted by Chris Satullo in Sojo.net, "Religious Right gives way to a new prophet," *The Philadelphia Inquirer*, February 19, 2008. Republished by *Sojourners*, accessed July 27, 2011, http://www.sojo.net/index.cfm?action=news.display_article&mode=s&NewsID=6542 (accessed 7/27/2011).

122. William Wilberforce, *A Practical View of Christianity* (New York, NY: Leavitt, Lord, & Co., 1835), Kindle edition.

123. John 3:16

124. John 12:3

125. John 12:6

126. Matthew 26:25, 49

127. John 6:70

128. J. C. Ryle, *The Gospel of John* (London: William Hunt and Company, 1856), Kindle edition.

129. John 12:8

130. Mark 14:7

131. R. C. Sproul, *John* (Wheaton, Il: Crossway, 2010), 219-220 (emphasis mine).

132. Revelation 21:4

133. 2 Corinthians 5:18-21

134. Corbett and Fikkert, *When Helping Hurts*, 115-119.

135. cf. 1 John 3:14

136. Matthew 25:31-46

137. Revelation 7:9-10

138. Ephesians 1:4

139. I encourage you to listen to Pastor Norm Millar's 2-part series

on finances, "Where is Your Treasure?" available at http://www.harvestlondon.ca/10194/blogentry/entry_id/210146/Where_is_Your_Treasure___Part_1 and http://www.harvestlondon.ca/10194/blogentry/entry_id/210838/Where_is_Your_Treasure__Part_2. This chapter owes a great debt to his excellent teaching.

140. cf. Romans 4:2, 1 Corinthians 3:21, Ephesians 2:9
141. Acts 2:22-24
142. Acts 2:37-41
143. Matthew 26:69-75, Luke 22:54-62, John 18:15-18
144. Acts 2:42-43
145. Acts 2:44-47, cf. 4:32-37
146. Exodus 25:2
147. Exodus 35:5, 36:5-7
148. 2 Corinthians 8:1-12
149. 2 Corinthians 9:6-12
150. James 2:14-17
151. 1 Timothy 5:8
152. Galatians 6:10
153. cf. Jeremiah 2:13, 17:13; John 4:10; Revelation 7:17
154. cf. Luke 21:2-4
155. Colossians 3:1-2
156. 1 Peter 1:3-4
157. 1 Corinthians 15:49
158. James 3:17, Galatians 4:26
159. Hebrews 4:16a, 1 Thessalonians 1:10a
160. Philippians 3:19b
161. Philippians 3:20-21
162. Christopher Wordsworth, *A Church History to the Council of Nicaea, A.D. 325* (Rivingtons, 1881), 465.
163. James Smith, *The Christian's Defence* (J.A. James, 1843), 37.
164. Revelation 21:5
165. Revelation 21:1-4
166. William Hendriksen, *More Than Conquerors: An Interpretation of the Book of Revelation* (Baker, 2007 [1940]), Kindle edition.
167. Timothy J. Keller, *Generous Justice: How God's Grace Makes Us Just* (New York, NY: Dutton, 2010), 113.
168. Revelation 7:16-17
169. Revelation 22:20

"But God..."
The Two Words at the Heart of the Gospel

by Casey Lute

**Just two words.
Understand their use in Scripture,
and you will never be the same.**

"Rock-solid theology packaged in an engaging and accessible form."
– **Louis Tullo, Sight Regained blog**

"Keying off of nine occurrences of "But God" in the English Bible, Casey Lute ably opens up Scripture in a manner that is instructive, edifying, encouraging, and convicting. This little book would be useful in family or personal reading, or as a gift to a friend. You will enjoy Casey's style, you will have a fresh view of some critical Scripture, and your appreciation for God's mighty grace will be deepened."
Dan Phillips, Pyromaniacs blog, author of _The World-Tilting Gospel_ (forthcoming from Kregel)

"A refreshingly concise, yet comprehensive biblical theology of grace that left this reader more in awe of the grace of God."
Aaron Armstrong, BloggingTheologically.com

""Casey Lute reminds us that nothing is impossible with God, that we must always reckon with God, and that God brings life out of death and joy out of sorrow."
Thomas R. Schreiner, Professor of New Testament Interpretation, The Southern Baptist Theological Seminary

"A mini-theology that will speak to the needs of every reader of this small but powerful book. Read it yourself and you will be blessed. Give it to a friend and you will be a blessing."
William Varner, Prof. of Biblical Studies, The Master's College

Reclaiming Adoption
Missional Living Through the Rediscovery of Abba Father

Dan Cruver, Editor
John Piper, Scotty Smith
Richard D. Phillips, Jason Kovacs

"There is no greater need in our day than theological clarity. Dan has brought us near to God's heart. As you read this book, you will sense the need to embrace your own acceptance as God's adopted child."
–Darrin Patrick, Pastor and author

"I can't recall ever hearing about, much less reading, a book like this before. Simply put, this remarkable volume fills a much-needed gap in our understanding of what the Bible says both about God's adoption of us and our adoption of others. I highly recommend it."
Sam Storms, Author of **The Singing God: Discover the Joy of Being Enjoyed by God**

"The authors writing here are some of the most fearless thinkers and activists in the Christian orphan care movement. Read. Be empowered. And then join Jesus for the orphans of the world."
Russell D. Moore, Pastor and author of **Adopted for Life**

"With spiritual insight and effective teaching, *Reclaiming Adoption* will help believers better understand our place with Christ and work in his kingdom."
Ed Stetzer, President, LifeWay Research

"Something like...a revival, is happening right now in evangelical theology....it may have the momentum to reinvigorate evangelical systematic theology....The most promising sign I've seen so far is the new book *Reclaiming Adoption*."
Fred Sanders, Ph.D., Biola University

Smooth Stones
Bringing Down the Giant
Questions of Apologetics

by Joe Coffey

Street-level apologetics for everyday Christians.

Because faith in Jesus makes sense. And you don't need an advanced degree to understand why.

"What a thrill for me to see Joe Coffey, a graduate of our first Centurions Program class, apply the biblical worldview principles we teach at BreakPoint and the Colson Center. In this marvelous little book, Joe simply and succinctly lays out the tenets of the Christian faith within the context of the four key life and worldview questions. This is an excellent resource for Christians and non-Christians alike who are seeking the Truth."
Chuck Colson, Founder of Prison Fellowship and the Colson Center for Christian Worldview

"This book may be the best resource I've seen to answer common objections in everyday language."
Jared Totten, **Critical Thinking Blog**

"A quick read that packs a punch....I'm always on the lookout for something like this. *Smooth Stones* is a winner."
Mike del Rosario, **ApologeticsGuy.Com**

"Most books on apologetics are too long, too deep, and too complicated. This book has none of these defects. Like its title, it is like a smooth stone from David's apologetic sling directed right to the mind of an enquiring reader"
Norman L. Geisler, Distinguished Professor of Apologetics, Veritas Evangelical Seminary, Murrieta, CA

Innocent Blood
Challenging the Powers of Death with the Gospel of Life

John Ensor

The shedding of innocent blood, primarily through abortion, has now marked an entire generation. But God's call to protect the innocent is unchanged. *We can obey that call.*

"God's Word tells us to be prepared to give an answer to everyone who asks us a reason for the hope within us, and it also tells us that we should do this with gentleness and respect. This book does just that. With decades of experience and true wisdom, John Ensor beautifully shows us how our glorious God delights in our courageous fight for the innocent, and that he commands us to fight, not with the words and weapons of man but with the living and active Gospel of Jesus Christ."
Burk Parsons, pastor; editor of Tabletalk

"...a powerful indictment. There are areas of theology about which sincere Christians can disagree, but this is not one of them."
John Frame, Professor, Reformed Theological Seminary

"By showing how our activism is to be motivated and fueled by the gospel, Ensor challenges us to devote our lives to magnifying Jesus Christ through seeking justice for the unborn."
Trevin Wax, author, editor at LifeWay Christian Resources

Stellar! John Ensor provides a bridge between the defense of innocent human life and the proclamation of the gospel. His concisely worded thesis is theologically grounded and philosophically sound. I wholeheartedly recommend this book!
Scott Klusendorf, speaker and author